Shakespeare
His Music and Song

LADY MARY SIDNEY WITH HER ARCHLUTE
(By kind permission of Lord de l'Isle & Dudley.)

Shakespeare
His Music and Song

By
A. H. Moncure-Sime

BENJAMIN BLOM, INC.
Publishers New York 1971

First published London, 1915
Reissued 1971 by
Benjamin Blom, Inc.
New York, N.Y. 10025

Library of Congress
Catalog Card Number 70-177518

Printed in the
United States of America

CONTENTS

CHAPTER I

CHAPTER II

CHAPTER III

CHAPTER IV

v

CHAPTER V

CHAPTER VI

CHAPTER VII

CONTENTS

CHAPTER VIII

CHAPTER IX

CHAPTER X

INTRODUCTORY

CHAPTER I

INTRODUCTORY

THE WORLD'S MAN

IN the long course of the world's history a few men have been born who seemed to assimilate and represent everything that was best in the particular age to which they belonged, and in the race among whom they lived. Each generation has its sons who o'ertop their fellows. It need not occasion us surprise that it should be so, though it is most difficult, if not impossible, to account for the genius or gifts of such men. Bright, eager, expectant spirits they are, uncommon to a degree, and alive in every fibre of their being. Then, on rare occasions, one is born who belongs not to a district but to the nation ; and still more rarely, one who belongs to mankind—a Universal. As Browning aptly puts it :

> 'A thousand poets pried at life,
> And only one amid the strife
> Rose to be Shakespeare'

3

SHAKESPEARE'S ENGLAND

It has been said, and with a great measure of truth, that Shakespeare 'was not of any age, but for all ages'; but in some respects the statement is misleading. By virtue of certain wonderful powers and perceptions he was certainly 'for all time', but he has certainly belonged peculiarly and distinctively to his own age, the Protestant and Monarchical age of Edmund Spencer, Ben Jonson, Bacon and Burleigh. As Edward Dowden remarks, 'A man does not attain to the universal by abandoning the particular, nor to the everlasting by an endeavour to overleap the limitations of time and place. The abiding reality exists not somewhere apart in the air, but under certain temporary and local forms of thought, feeling, and endeavour. We come most deeply into communication with the permanent facts and forces of human nature and human life, by accepting first of all this fact, that a definite point of observation and sympathy, not a vague nowhere, has been assigned to each of us'.

It was a very practical, positive England into which Shakespeare was born in 1564. England was then developing into a great Protestant Power. In 1587, Mary, Queen of Scots, was executed, and the breach between England

and the Catholic world was irrevocable and complete. In the following year Spain sought to punish and humiliate England by fitting up her great Armada, and sending into European waters the largest fleet that had ever been seen there. England was equal and more than equal to the occasion, and Spain's attempt to crush her rival's growing power was met with utmost discomfiture. Naturally enough, England revelled in the sense of victory. Her star was in the ascendant. The country was eminently prosperous in every direction, and the men and women of the times were peculiarly alert, strenuous and daring. The leaders were wise and courageous, sound and vigorous. As George Brandes puts it, 'They knew how to rule with courage and wisdom, like the Queen and Lord Burghley ; how to live nobly and fight gloriously, to love with passion and sing with enthusiasm, like the beautiful hero of the younger generation, Sir Philip Sidney, who found an early Achilles-death'. In a sentence, the people of England as a whole were bent on the enjoyment of a full life, a life in which all the senses were actively employed, a life which had room in it for wit as well as for wisdom, for contemplation as well as the widest conquering activity. It was in Shakespeare's day that England's now world-wide commerce and industry came into being. Before that time Antwerp had been the centre of the world's commerce, but during Elizabeth's reign London took that proud position, and continues to hold it. The Royal Exchange was opened in 1571, and in a quarter of a century from that date the English had appropriated a large part of the commerce which had until then been in the possession of Hamburg and the other towns of the Hanseatic League.

While England's naval and military power had advanced by leaps and bounds, and while her commerce had made great strides, there had also been a great and wonderful Renascence of Learning. While travellers and explorers brought back their stories of adventure from distant foreign parts, scholars at home had been making voyages into the realm of Letters. The world had suddenly become a vast place, with wide and ever-widening horizon, and the minds of men were filled with a great hope. As the truest representative of his age, therefore, we might reasonably expect that the Drama of Shakespeare should teem with vigorous vitality. In these plays he brings us a vision of Life in all its varied aspects. 'We are shown the strong man taken in the toils; the sinner sinking farther and farther away from light and reality, and the substantial life of things, into the dubious and the dusk ; the pure heart all vital, and confident, and joyous ; we are shown the glad, vicarious sacrifice of soul for soul, the malign activity of evil, the vindication of right by the true justiciary ; we are shown the good common things of the world, and the good things that are rare ; the love of parents and children, the comradeship of young men, the exquisite vivacity, courage, and high-spirited intellect of noble girlhood, the devotion of man and woman to man and woman '. He brings us the vision, and we know that the vision represents what is perfectly true and real.

It was a great and vital age in which Shakespeare lived and wrote, and he was truly and supremely representative of his age. As Walter Bagehot says, ' When you read him you feel a sensation of motion, a conviction that there is something " up ", a notion that not only is something being talked about, but also that something is being done '. He was the representative man of a period when it was the special craving of the people of England to give vent to their feelings, to satisfy their eye and heart, ' to set free boldly on all the roads of existence the pack of appetites and instincts '. In his works this whole striving, expanding, rising world is unfolded.

THE POET'S GIFTS

There is evermore a rich reward for those who study the great poets aright. They furnish us with ideals. Whether in colour or form, or sound or words, or if there be any other form or medium of communication, the poets present to us that which liberates us for the time being from the finite. He awakens the infinite. He makes us feel that we have a soul. If it were not for the poets in their various capacity, we should as good as die. When we strip life of its poetry, only the dreariest blank remains. No longer do the little ones play their games or tell their fairy stories, and men and women lose faith and hope and love in what they say and think and do. But the true poet comes along, then the music speaks, the colours thrill, the children engage in games of merry fancy, and men and women learn to hope and love. The study of Shakespeare is the study of the soul in all its moods. It has been said that a 'principal character of the works of a very great author is, that in them each man can find that for which he seeks, and in a form which includes his own view'. This remark is certainly most true in the case of Shakespeare. The literary artist, the philosopher, the ethicist, all come to him and each is eminently satisfied with the treatment of his own pet subject. It is the same with the one who is interested in and loves music. In these plays he finds many references to music and musical instruments, and he cannot help being astonished at the completeness and accuracy which the Poet displays in dealing with this as with every subject he takes in hand.

The Bard of Avon

The true poet is a historian, a painter, and a musician all in one. The Greek legend has it that a Greek girl tracing the shadow of her lover's face on a sunny wall gave rise to the art of painting. And the death of one of the great heroes of an ancient world may have been the occasion of the rise of the twin arts of poetry and music. The hero of the barbaric long-ago returning to his native village laden with the spoils of some great chase, or driving before him a horde of captives, must have a poet to rehearse his triumphs, to set down in stirring song the strength of his mighty arm and the terrors of his unconquerable spear. To some such source hidden in the mists of antiquity we may trace back the sacred streams of poetry and music which have flowed down to us out of unknown time. And from his power of conferring a new distinction on heroic achievements, the bard or singer has ever been held in honour. His poems are themselves a kind of rude fame, a roll of glory. We find the bard in every nation and in every age; and everywhere he is regarded as one worthy of the obeisance of his less gifted compatriots. The Bard of Avon was conspicuously gifted, and as Swinburne says: 'It is not only the crowning glory of England, it is the crowning glory of mankind that such a man should ever have been born as William Shakespeare'.

As an author, Shakespeare was not merely with men, but of men; he was not a thing apart, with a clear intuition of what was in those around him; he must have had in his own nature the germs and tendencies of those very elements that he has so graphically and sympathetically described. He knew what was in the human heart, for he felt it in himself. Throughout all his writings we find what some critics have called an excessive tendency to dwell on the common features of very ordinary lives. For every one of his characters there is the firm ground of humanity, upon which the weeds as well as the flowers, glorious or fantastic as the case may be, show themselves. His greatly heroic characters, such as Hamlet, Lady Macbeth, Shylock, and King Lear, are the most profoundly human.

It is our National Bard's unique distinction that he
had an absolute command over all the complexi-
ties of thought and feeling that prompt to action,
and bring out the dividing lines of character. He
swept with the hand of a Master the whole
gamut of human experience, from the lowest note
to the very top of the compass, from, as it has
been put, ' the sportive treble of Mamilius and
the pleading boyish tones of Prince Arthur, up
to the spectre-haunted terrors of Macbeth, the
tropical passion of Othello, the agonized senses
and tortured spirit of Hamlet, the sustained ele-
mental grandeur, the Titanic force and utterly
tragical pathos of Lear '. Swinburne asserts, not
too extravagantly surely, that ' of good and evil,
in all their subtlest and sublimest forms of thought
and action and revelation, he (Shakespeare)
knew more than ever it has been given to any
other man to know ; no child of man and woman
was too high or too low for his perfect apprehen-
sion and appreciation '.

As a creator in literature who without doubt
possessed surpassing knowledge, who had mysterious kinship with the elements, and who in solitary
places heard the messages of the gods, it is not
to be wondered at, but rather to be expected,
that there should be a great deal about Music
and Song in the Plays and Poetry of Shakespeare.

Such hints, allusions, similes, and moralizings
are not only natural but inevitable in the writings
of one who is a mouthpiece, so to speak, for
Humanity.

MUSIC AND THE
MAN
MUSIC AS UNIFIER

CHAPTER II

*Music (writes Thomas Carlyle) is well said to be
the speech of angels : in fact, nothing among the
utterances allowed to mankind is felt to be so divine.
It brings us near to the Infinite ; we look for moments,
across the cloudy elements, into the eternal Sea of
Light, when song leads and inspires us. Serious
nations, all nations that can still listen to the mandate
of Nature, have prized song and music as the highest :
as a vehicle for worship, for prophecy, and for whatso-
ever in them was divine. Their singer was a* vates,
*admitted to the council of the universe, friend of the
gods, and choicest benefactor to man.*

The Opera (Critical Essays, Vol. IV)

MUSIC AND THE MAN

MUSIC in one form or another—it may be
very primitive or most highly developed
—is a language which is universal in its appeal.
Men of every race and colour, men of all stages
of learning, appreciate more or less the message
it lays on the common heart, and respond in a
greater or less extent to its influence. Whatever
the scientific explanation may be, it is a fact be-

15

yond dispute that man responds to rhythmical
sounds. In the savage, music is probably little
more than an impulse towards rhythmic sound;
while in the cultured composer of our highly
civilized age it is an expression of a refined emotional state, through the complex language of
musical notation.

As Mr. W. S. Lilly says: 'No doubt every
great poet is a great teacher. But his teaching
is as the teaching of Nature herself: unpre-
meditated, unreasoned, undefined; like the
sound of the sea, or the fragrance of flowers, or
the sweet influences of the stars. Like Nature,
poets—according to Plato's most true *dictum*—
utter great and wise things which they do not
themselves understand. The songs of Apollo are
as inspired as his oracles. The poet, " soaring
in the high reason of his fancies ", like the priestess
on her tripod, speaks not of himself'.

Another fact about Music to attract the attention of anyone at all interested in the subject
is that as one of the arts it is quite peculiarly
adaptable to the various needs of man. However enthusiastically devoted we may be to other
forms of art—to Painting or to Sculpture—we can
hardly deny that there is a far wider and far more
intelligent appreciation of Music than of the two
sister arts we have named. In every form of

Social life—in the home, in the Church, and in the theatre—there is abundant proof of its wonderful adaptability to the needs of humanity. It must have been quite patent to Shakespeare that Music had the power to lead all to one common meeting ground of temper and prepare the minds of all for unanimity of thought and action by a unanimity of feeling.

As bearing on this point, the following leaderette from *The Manchester Guardian* of December 11, 1915, is interesting :

MUSIC AS UNIFIER

' If there could be any doubt about the wisdom of Mr (now Sir Thomas) Beecham in identifying our musical policy largely with the streams of national and allied enthusiasm, the invitation of Mr Beecham to Rome to conduct a great musical festival intended to celebrate and foster the political enthusiasms of the Allied Nations would demonstrate the soundness of his judgment. The idea that the arts are a thing apart and have no more than a symbolical relation to our immediate life is only one of the fictions which a false reverence for the art of the past makes us believe. The work of the artist is first of all to celebrate our present life, and at supreme moments like the present, this duty of the artist becomes not less but more imperative. The art of music is especially suitable not only for all ceremonial occasions, but public music is in itself a kind of ceremony which stimulates feeling and binds people together. In devoting himself to promote an understanding and appreciation of each other's music among the Allied Nations Mr Beecham is working towards that unity of feeling which is above all things necessary to achieve our common purpose in the war. Manchester people may well take a pride in the fact that the music for the forthcoming festival in Rome, imposing and full of novelty as it is, and thoroughly representative of the Allied Nations is after all little more than a *replica* of the good things we have had in Manchester since the war began '.

Professor Dowden in his classical book on *Shakespeare : His Mind and Art,* calls attention to the nothing less than marvellous powers of acquisition which the National Poet possessed. He points out that quite a little library exists to illustrate the minute acquaintance of Shakespeare with this branch of information and with that : *The Legal Acquirements of Shakespeare, Shakespeare's Knowledge and Use of the Bible, Shakespeare's Delineations of Insanity, The Rural Life of Shakespeare, Shakespeare's Garden, The Ornithology of Shakespeare, The Insects mentioned*

by Shakespeare, and such like.   All these special
critical studies of Shakespeare prove the astounding receptivity of the poet's mind.   When we
come to examine closely Shakespeare's treatment
of Music in his works we can hardly help being
amazed at its fullness and variety.   Dr Edward
M. Naylor, in his masterly little book on *Shakespeare and Music*, makes reference in the index
to thirty-three plays and four poems, and deals
with nearly two hundred and thirty passages
which not only speak of Music, but in many
instances present difficulties, or render necessary
to the ordinary reader the services of some
expert.   On the authority of the same author
we may take it for granted that there are no fewer
than five hundred passages in Shakespeare's
works, dealing more or less directly with Music
or musical instruments.

In the following chapters we shall speak of
some of the many allusions to Music, Song,
Dance, and Musical Instruments in these immortal Plays.

THE TEMPEST
TWELFTH NIGHT
AS YOU LIKE IT

CHAPTER III

Shakespeare is the king of poetic rhythm and style, as well as the king of the realm of thought; along with his dazzling prose, Shakespeare has succeeded in giving us the most varied, the most harmonious verse which has ever sounded upon the human ear since the verse of the Greeks.

Henry Cochin.

THE TEMPEST

WITH two or three exceptions, music and singing play quite an important part in the Comedies of Shakespeare. In *The Tempest* the use that is made of Music is wholly admirable, and in the descriptions of its enchanting and disenchanting effects delightfully apt. The appearances of Ariel are invariably accompanied with music which is daintily described and introduced with the most artistic fitness.

Many attempts have been made to place *The Tempest* among the early plays of Shakespeare, but most reliable critics are strongly inclined to the idea that it is one of his latest. There are many points of comparison between what is well known to have been one of his early dramas,

A Midsummer Night's Dream, and this, probably,
his last.   There is about them both a common
atmosphere of romance and magic ; the intrigues
in both are delightfully improbable and absurd ;
and the studied contrasts of the grotesque with the
refined, the ethereal with the earthly, are very
marked.

One writer on *The Tempest* says that Ariel
is comparable to the fantasy of Shakespeare, ' a
light tissue of bold inventions, of ardent passions,
melancholy mockery, dazzling poetry '. ' Nothing could be more like the poet's mind than
these nimble *genii*, children of air and flame,
whose flights " compass the globe in a second ",
who glide over the foam of the waves and slip
between the atoms of the wind.   Ariel flies, an
invisible songster, around shipwrecked men to
console them, discovers the thoughts of traitors,
pursues the savage beast Caliban, spreads gorge-
ous visions before lovers, and does all in a lightning-
flash '.

Learned attempts have been made to fix the
longitude and latitude of the Scene of Action of
this Play, but surely all such investigation is
needless and useless.   ' All these dreams of
Shakespeare are divine phantasms, and shadows
of things that are '.   We agree with Mr G. L.
Strachey, who, writing in *The Independent Re-*

view, said : 'In *The Tempest*, unreality has reached its apotheosis. Two of the principal characters are frankly not human beings at all ; and the whole action passes, through a series of impossible occurrences, in a place which can only by courtesy be said to exist. The Enchanted Island, indeed, peopled, for a timeless moment, by this strange fantastic medley of persons and of things, has been cut adrift for ever from common sense, and floats, buoyed up by a sea, not of waters, but of poetry. Never did Shakespeare's magnificence of diction reach more marvellous heights than in some of the speeches of Prospero, or his lyric art a purer beauty than in the songs of Ariel '. (Page 415, August, 1904.)

Many and varied are the allusions to Music, vocal and instrumental, in this delightful and fantastic play. In Act I, sc. 2, Ariel, invisible, playing and singing, sings the following song :

> Come unto these yellow sands,
>   And then take hands ;
> Courtsied when you have and kiss'd
>   The wild waves whist :
> Foot it featly here and there ;
> And, sweet sprites, the burthen bear.
>   Hark, hark !
>   *Burthen* (*dispersedly*) : Bow-wow.

Ariel: The watch-dogs bark:
>   *Burthen (dispersedly):* Bow-wow.

Ariel: Hark, hark! I hear
The strain of strutting chanticleer
Cry, Cock-o-diddle-dow.

Ferdinand: Where should this music be?
>   i' th' air or th' earth?

It sounds no more: and, sure, it waits upon
Some god o' th' island. Sitting on a bank,
Weeping again the king my father's wreck,
This music crept by me upon the waters,
Allaying both their fury and my passion
With its sweet air: thence I have follow'd it,
Or it hath drawn me rather. But 'tis gone.
No, it begins again.

Ariel then sings the strangely tender, moving
song, *Full Fathom Five:*

>   Full fathom five thy father lies;
>   Of his bones are coral made;
>   Those are pearls that were his eyes:
>   Nothing of him that doth fade,
>   But doth suffer a sea-change
>   Into something rich and strange.
>   Sea-nymphs hourly ring his knell:
>   *Burthen:* Ding-dong.

Ariel: Hark! now I hear them,—Ding-dong,
bell.

Ferd. : The ditty doth remember my drown'd
  father.
This is no mortal business, nor no sound
That the earth owes :—I hear it now above me.

The original settings of most of these beautiful
old melodies have been lost, but we are fortunate
in having a setting of this song by one Johnson,
dating back to 1612.

A snatch of song is sung by Ariel into the ear
of honest old Gonzalo :

> While you here do snoring lie,
> Open-ey'd conspiracy
>   His time doth take.
> If of life you keep a care,
> Shake off slumber, and beware :
>   Awake, awake !
>
> (Act II, sc. 1.)

Stephano, one of the three rascals in the Play,
treats us in Act II, sc. 2, to some of the ribald,
vulgar music which was no doubt very prevalent
in the tavern company of the times.

Steph. : I shall no more to sea, to sea,
  Here shall I die a-shore.
This is a very scurvy tune to sing at a man's
  funeral : well, here's my comfort.
    (Sings)   *(Drinks)*

The master, the swabber, the boatswain, and I
    The gunner, and his mate,
Loved Moll, Meg, and Marian, and Margery,
    But none of us cared for Kate ;
    For she had a tongue with a tang,
    Would cry to a sailor, Go hang !
She lov'd not the savour of tar nor of pitch ;
Yet a tailor might scratch her where'er she did
    itch.
    Then, to sea, boys, and let her go hang !
This is a scurvy tune, too : but here's mv
    comfort.

                                        (*Drinks*)

   The following grotesque ditty is howled out
by Caliban when in a drunken mood. (Act II,
sc. 2) :

Farewell, master ; farewell, farewell !
    No more dams I'll make for fish ;
        Nor fetch in firing
        At requiring ;
    Nor scrape trencher, nor wash dish :
        'Ban 'Ban, Ca—Caliban,
        Has a new master :—get a new man.
Freedom, hey-day ! hey-day ! freedom ! freedom,
    hey-day, freedom !

   In Act III, sc. 2, we have one of the many

cases of Catch-singing in Shakespeare. Caliban
asks Stephano to ' troll the Catch ' which he had
been teaching him some little time before.

Steph.: At thy request, monster, I will do
　reason, any reason,
Come on, Trinculo, let us sing.　(*Sings*)
　　Flout 'em and scout 'em,
　　And scout 'em and flout 'em;
　　　Thought is free.
Caliban: That's not the tune.

(Ariel plays the tune on a tabor and pipe)

Steph.: What is this same ?
Trin.: This is the tune of our Catch, played
by the picture of Nobody.
Steph.: If thou beest a man, show thyself in
thy likeness : if thou beest a devil, take 't as thou
list.
Trin.: O, forgive me my sins !
Steph.: He that dies pays all debts : I defy
thee.　Mercy upon us !
Cal.: Art thou afeard ?
Steph.: No, monster, not I.
Cal.: Be not afeard ; the isle is full of noises,
Sounds and sweet airs, that give delight, and hurt
　not.
Sometimes a thousand twangling instruments

Will hum about mine ears; and sometime voices,
That, if I then had waked after long sleep,
Will make me sleep again: and then, in dreaming,
The clouds methought would open, and show
    riches
Ready to drop upon me; that, when I waked,
I cried to dream again.
    Steph.: This will prove a brave kingdom to
    me, where
I shall have my music for nothing.

In Act IV, sc. 1, we are treated to a kind of
duet with Juno and Ceres as the singers. They
sing.
    Juno: Honour, riches, marriage-blessing,
Long continuance and increasing,
Hourly joys be still upon you!
Juno sings her blessings on you.
    Ceres: Earth's increase, foison plenty,
Barns and garners never empty;
Vines with cheering bunches growing;
Plants with goodly burthens bowing;
Spring come to you at the farthest
In the very end of harvest!
Scarcity and want shall shun you;
Ceres' blessing so is on you.

In the last Act, in response to Prospero's call for
'A solemn air, and the best comforter to an

unsettled fancy ', Ariel sings the melody which has
charmed so many generations in the past, and
has lost none of its fascination for us to-day.

Where the bee sucks, there suck I :
In a cowslip's bell I lie ;
There I couch when owls do cry.
On a bat's back I do fly
After summer merrily.
Merrily, merrily shall I live now
Under the blossom that hangs on the bough.

So ends this dainty, haunting, fantastic, lyrical
romance—one of the most wonderful and success-
ful excursions, surely, ever made into the realm
of ' unreasoning and creative imagination '.

TWELFTH NIGHT

Twelfth Night is probably the last of the joyous
comedies, holding a middle place between *As
You Like It* and *All's Well*. The Play opens with
a very beautiful eulogy on Music, and the sentiment of Music breathes throughout.

Act I, sc. 1

Duke of Illyria : If music be the food of love,
   play on ;
Give me excess of it, that, surfeiting,
The appetite may sicken, and so die.
That strain again' it had a dying fall :

O, it came o'er my ear like the sweet sound,
That breathes upon a bank of violets!
Stealing and giving odour! Enough; no more!
'Tis not so sweet as it was before.

Then *Viola* says:

I'll serve this Duke:
Thou shalt present me as an eunuch to him:
It may be worth thy pains; for I can sing,
And speak to him in many sorts of music
That will allow me very worth his service.

The Duke's sensibility to the power of Music
is very strikingly disclosed in his interview with
Viola (line 32, Act I, sc. 4):

thy small pipe
Is as the maiden's organ, shrill and sound.

Act II, sc. 3

Sir Andrew Aguecheek asks the Clown for a
song, and compliments him on his singing the
previous evening. The Clown obliges by singing:

O mistress mine, where are you roaming?
O stay and hear, your true love's coming,
That can sing both high and low:
Trip no farther, pretty sweeting;
Journeys end in lovers meeting,
Every wise man's son doth know.[1]

[1] The Music of this is given on page 178.

And then :

> What is love ? 'tis not hereafter ;
> Present mirth hath present laughter ;
>   What's to come is still unsure :
> In delay there lies no plenty ;
> Then come kiss me, sweet and twenty,
>   Youth's a stuff will not endure.

Sir Toby Belch then suggests that they ' make the welkin dance indeed ', and ' rouse the night-owl in a catch that will draw three souls out of one weaver '. They all lustily take up the catch which Maria likens to ' caterwauling ', and Malvolio describes as ' gabbling like tinkers '.

The scraps of songs and catches bawled out by Sir Andrew, Sir Toby, and the Clown were no doubt quite well-known and popular ditties in the time of Shakespeare.

The Duke is very constant in his passion for Music, as constant for it as for Olivia, and in the fourth scene of this same Act he again asks for Music.

> Give me some music. Now, good morrow, friends,
> Now, good Cesarto, but that piece of song,
> That old and antique song we heard last night :
> Methought it did relieve my passion much,

More than light airs and recollected terms
Of these most brisk and giddy-paced times:
Come, but one verse.

The song had been sung by the jester Feste
who was brought into the Duke's presence and
requested to repeat the song. The Duke comments on the song as follows:

Mark it Cesarto, it is old and plain;
The spinsters and the knitters in the sun
And the free maids that weave their thread with
        bones
Do use to chant it: it is silly sooth,
And dallies with the innocence of love,
Like the old age.

Then the Jester sings:

Come away, come away, death,
And in sad cypress let me be laid;
Fly away, fly away, breath;
I am slain by a fair cruel maid.
My shroud of white, stuck all with yew,
        O, prepare it!
My part of death, no one so true
    . Did share it.
Not a flower, not a flower sweet,
On my black coffin let there be strown;

Not a friend, not a friend greet
My poor corpse, where my bones shall be thrown :
A thousand thousand sighs to save,
    Lay me, O, where
Sad true lover never find my grave,
    To weep there.

On two more occasions at least the Jester or Clown sings, in Act IV, sc. 2, when he introduces the song—

    I am gone, sir,
    And anon, sir,
    I'll be with you again,
    In a trice,
    Like to the old vice,
    Your need to sustain ;
    Who, with dagger of lath,
    In his rage and his wrath
    Cries, ah, ha ! to the devil :
    Like a mad lad,
    Pare thy nails, dad ;
    Adieu, goodman devil.

And in the pretty and popular song which serves as an epilogue to this wholly delightful play :

When that I was and a tiny little boy,
    With hey, ho, the wind and the rain,

A foolish thing was but a toy,
  For the rain it raineth every day.
But when I came to man's estate,
  With hey, ho, the wind and the rain,
'Gainst knaves and thieves men shut their gate,
  For the rain it raineth every day.
But when I came, alas! to wive,
  With hey, ho, the wind and the rain,
By swaggering could I never thrive,
  For the rain it raineth every day.
But when I came unto my beds,
  With hey, ho, the wind and the rain,
With toss-pots still had drunken heads,
  For the rain it raineth every day.
A great while ago the world began,
  With hey, ho, the wind and the rain,
But that's all one, our play is done,
  And we'll strive to please you every day.

As You Like it

The first reference to Music which we find in
As You Like It, is Rosalind's pun on the Duke's
wrestler when he has broken the ribs of several
of his opponents.

Act I, sc. 2: 'But is there any else longs to
see this broken music in his sides?'

Repeated reference is made in these plays to 'broken music'. The best explanation of the term seems to be that given by Elson : 'The employment of the instruments, either in accompanying vocal music, or in purely instrumental forms, had one peculiar restriction in the sixteeth and seventeenth centuries. It was the habit of keeping each family of instruments by itself in a " consort ". Thus there could be a " consort of viols ", a " consort of hautboys ", but if one kind of instrument entered into a " consort " of other instruments than those of its own family, the result was called " broken music " '.

In using the metaphor ' broken music ' in the above-quoted passage the Poet is of course playing upon words, just as we find him doing in *King Henry V*. When the King is wooing Queen Katharine he says, ' Come, your answer in broken music ; for thy voice is music and thy English broken ; therefore, queen of all, Katharine, break thy mind to me in broken English. Wilt thou have me ? ' (Act V, sc. 2).

In Act II we have a framework of musical talk around the charming and well-known song (sc. 5), *Under the Greenwood Tree*, which is sung by Amiens :

> Under the greenwood tree
> Who loves to lie with me,

And tune his merry note
Unto the sweet bird's throat,
Come hither, come hither, come hither:
Here shall he see
No enemy
But winter and rough weather.

When Amiens has sung one verse, Jaques calls for more; and though the singer pleads a ragged voice, and inability to give any pleasure by his singing, Jaques insists, saying that it is not pleasure he wants but the music of the song. So Amiens sings a second verse, as follows:

Who doth ambition shun,

(*all together here*),

And loves to live i' the sun,
Seeking the food he eats,
And pleased with what he gets,
Come hither, come hither, come hither:
etc., etc.

Jaques himself provides the third and last verse which runs as follows:

If it do come to pass
That any man turn ass,
Leaving his wealth and ease
A stubborn will to please,

> Ducdame, ducdame, ducdame:
>   Here shall he see
>   Gross fools as he,
> And if he will come to me.

Much learned comment has been expended on the word 'ducdame', but as it is not germane to our subject, we content ourselves by referring any curious reader to the Variorum Edition of Shakespeare by Furness, vol. viii, pp. 97-9, where he will find a great deal of very interesting if not particularly convincing material.

In sc. 7 of Act II, after the glorious period of Jaques on the Seven Ages of man, the Duke calls for music. His good cousin Amiens sings:

> Blow, blow, thou winter wind,
> Thou art not so unkind
>   As man's ingratitude;
> Thy touch is not so keen,
> Because thou art not seen,
>   Although thy breath be rude.

> Heigh-ho! sing, heigh-ho! unto the green holly:
> Most friendship is feigning, most loving mere
>   folly:
>   Then, heigh-ho, the holly!
>   This life is most jolly.

Freeze, freeze, thou bitter sky,
That dost not bite so nigh
  As benefits forgot:
Though thou the waters warp,
Thy sting is not so sharp
  As friend remember'd not.

Heigh-ho! sing, etc.

In sc. 2 of Act IV we have one of the numerous hunting songs found in these plays. Jaques says to the forester, 'Have you no song, forester, for this purpose?' meaning a song wherewith to celebrate the prowess of the man who had killed the deer. Then four foresters sing the Round or Catch, as follows:

What shall he have that kill'd the deer?
His leather skin and horns to wear.
  Then sing him home:
      (*The rest shall bear this burden.*)
Take thou no scorn to wear the horn;
It was a crest ere thou wast born;
  Thy father's father wore it,
  And thy father bore it:
All: The horn, the horn, the lusty horn
Is not a thing to laugh to scorn.

Some eminent authorities contend that the words partially in brackets, 'The rest shall bear this burden ' have nothing to do with the play proper, but are merely a direction to the singers to join in the ' burden ' of the song.

It has been pointed out that some characters are introduced forcibly and without any apparent reason into Shakespeare's plays, but that their presence will be readily understood if we remember that three were necessary to sing the Catch music which the poet wished to introduce. Such a character is introduced in the third scene of the fifth Act of this Play. Audrey and Touchstone are together. Two pages come in, and we soon gather why they have walked upon the stage.

Touch. : By my troth, well met. Come, sit, sit, and a song.

Sec. Page : We are for you : sit t' the middle.

First Page : Shall we clap into't roundly, without hawking or spitting or saying we are hoarse, which are the only prologues to a bad voice ?

Sec. Page : I' faith, i' faith ; and both in a tune, like two gipsies on a horse.

Then follows the ever-favourite song, ' It was a Lover and his Lass ', the original setting of which is in Advocate's Library, Edinburgh, and bears the date 1639.

It was a lover and his lass,
    With a hey, and a ho, and a hey nonino,
That o'er the green corn-field did pass
    In the spring time, the only pretty ring time
When birds do sing, hey ding a ding, ding:
Sweet lovers love the spring.

Between the acres of the rye,
    With a hey, and a ho, and a hey nonino,
These pretty country folks would lie,
    In spring time, etc.

This carol they began that hour,
    With a hey, and a ho, and a hey nonino,
How that a life was but a flower
    In spring time, etc.

And therefore take the present time,
    With a hey, and a ho, and a hey nonino;
For love is crowned with the prime
    In spring time, etc.

Touch. : Truly, young gentleman, though there was no great matter in the ditty, yet the note was very untuneable.

First Page : You are deceived, sir; we kept time, we lost not our time.

Touch. : By my troth, yes; I count it but time lost to hear such a foolish song. God be wi'

you; and God mend your voices! Come,
Audrey.

In the last scene of the last Act there is a little
wedding song.

> Wedding is great Juno's crown :
>   O blessed bond of board and bed !
> 'Tis Hymen peoples every town ;
>   High wedlock then be honoured :
> Honour, high honour and renown,
> To Hymen, god of every town !

LOVE'S LABOUR'S
  LOST
THE WINTER'S TALE
A MIDSUMMER
  NIGHT'S DREAM

CHAPTER IV

Shakespeare's mind contained within itself the germs of all faculty and feeling. . . . So mighty a faculty sets at nought the common limitations of nationality, and in every quarter of the globe to which civilized life has penetrated, Shakespeare's power is recognized. . . . Hamlet and Othello, Lear and Macbeth, Falstaff and Shylock, Brutus and Romeo, Ariel and Caliban are studied in almost every civilized tongue as if they were historic personalities, and the chief of the impressive phrases that fall from their lips are rooted in the speech of civilized humanity.

Sir Sidney Lee.

Love's Labour's Lost

LOVE'S Labour's Lost has been compared to Comic Opera. Its lyrical character is one of its most noteworthy features. The experts place it first of the plays of the rhyming period. In the form in which we now have it, it contains twice as many rhymed lines as blank verse, and probably in its original state the proportion may have been greater. While this Play only provides us with two songs, it contains an immense amount of doggerel and alternate rhymes. Dr Johnson thinks that a song has apparently been lost from Act III, sc. 1, where the Author tells us there is singing. What a beautiful and comprehensive request is here made by Armado. 'Warble, child'; (speaking to Moth) 'make passionate my sense of hearing.' None of the fine arts can subsist or give rapture, without passion. Hence mediocrity in painting, sculpture, or music, is more intolerable than in any of the other Arts. Music, when not of the best in form and execution, and without any high fervour or passion, is apt to be monotonous as the tolling of a bell or the antics of a clown.

There are a good many references to dances and an allusion to a notable ballad in this Play.

When Armado tells Moth to warble, the Page does so, and the air he sings is 'Concolinel', the song which as suggested above has been lost.

Armado : Sweet air !—Go, tenderness of years ; take this key, give enlargement to the swain, bring him festinately hither. I must employ him in a letter to my love.

Moth : Master, will you win your love with a French brawl ?

Arm. : How meanest thou ? brawling in French ?

Moth : No, my complete master ; but to jig off a tune at the tongue's end, canary to it with your feet, humour it with turning up your eyelids, sigh a note and sing a note, sometimes through the throat, as if you swallowed love with singing love, sometime through the nose, as if you snuffed up love by smelling love ; with your hat pent-house-like o'er the shop of your eyes ; with your arms crossed on your thin-belly doublet, like a rabbit on a spit ; or your hands in your pockets, like a man after the old painting, and keep not too long in one tune, but a snip and away. These are compliments, these are humours ; these betray nice wenches, that would be betrayed without these ; and make them men of note—do you note me ?—that most are affected to these.

The Brawl was one of several tunes to which the Country Dance was danced, whether in a ring, or 'at length', like our 'Sir Toby'. Brawl was the English of the French 'bransle' or 'branle'. Like the Allemande of Bach, 'it containeth the time of eight, and most commonly in short notes'.

The Canary was a fairly quick dance, and its rhythm was generally 6–8 time. There is no history of the name, but Skeat thinks it probably derived its name from the Canary Islands. This dance is referred to in two other Plays, and the allusions make clear the lively character of the dance.

It is in this Play that the only mention is made by Shakespeare of the Round country-dance, so loved by the rustics—the Hey, Hay, or Haye. The allusion is in Act V, sc. 1, where the account is given of the preparation for the Pageant of the Worthies. The Hay was a very lively, even boisterous dance. 'The performers stood in a circle to begin with, and then "wind round handing in passing until you come to your places"'.

The Morrice, or Morris Dance was very popular in Shakespeare's time, and he introduces it into this Play—when Holofernes says to the country wench Jaquenetta, 'Trip and go, my sweet'. 'Trip and Go' was one of the liveliest of morris-dances. Many of the old dances were sung, and Elson suggests that the very word 'ballad' may have been derived from *ballare* (Italian), to dance. The old song-dances sometimes went by the name of 'ballets'.

The allusion which Shakespeare makes to one of the notable old ballads is in Act I, sc. 2, when Armado asks Moth if there is not a ballad of the King and the Beggar? Moth replies, 'The

world was very guilty of such a ballad some
three ages since : but, I think, now 'tis not to be
found ; or, if it were, it would neither serve for
the writing nor the tune '.

Armado says he will have the subject ' newly
writ o'er ', and he certainly kept his promise,
for his declaration of love which follows is taken
bodily from the old ballad, *A Song of a Beggar
and a King*.

In sc. 2 of Act V we have two songs, one to be
sung by Ver, the spring, and the other to be
maintained by Hiems, winter. The former is
the well-known :

When daisies pied, and violets blue,
    And lady-smocks all silver-white,
And cuckoo-buds of yellow hue,
    Do paint the meadows with delight,
The cuckoo then, on every tree,
Mocks married men ; for thus sings he,
        Cuckoo ;
Cuckoo, cuckoo : O word of fear,
Unpleasing to a married ear !

When shepherds pipe on oaten straws,
    And merry larks are ploughmen's clocks,
When turtles tread, and rooks, and daws,
    And maidens bleach their summer smocks,

The cuckoo then, on every tree,
    Mocks married men ; for thus sings he,
        Cuckoo ;
Cuckoo, cuckoo : O word of fear,
Unpleasing to a married ear !

And the latter is :

When icicles hang by the wall,
    And Dick the shepherd blows his nail,
And Tom bears logs into the hall,
    And milk comes frozen home in pail,
When blood is nipp'd and ways be foul,
    Then nightly sings the staring owl,
        Tu-whit ;
Tu-who, a merry note,
While greasy Joan doth keel the pot.

When all aloud the wind doth blow,
    And coughing drowns the parson's saw,
And birds sit brooding in the snow,
    And Marian's nose looks red and raw,
When roasted crabs hiss in the bowl,
    Then nightly sings the staring owl,
        Tu-whit ;
Tu-who, a merry note,
While greasy Joan doth keel the pot.

The Winter's Tale

There are few songs or musical allusions in
this Play.   In Act IV, sc. 2 we have two trifling,
nonsensical ditties from the lips of that rogue and
trifler Autolycus :

When daffodils begin to peer,
 With heigh ! the doxy over the dale,
Why, then comes in the sweet o' the year ;
 For the red blood reigns in the winter's pale.

The white sheet bleaching on the hedge,
 With heigh ! the sweet birds, O, how they sing !
Doth set my pugging tooth on edge ;
 For a quart of ale is a dish for a king.

The lark, that tirra-lyra chants,
 With heigh ! with heigh ! the thrush and the
  jay,
Are summer songs for me and my aunts,
 While we lie tumbling in the hay.

I have served Florizel, and in my time wore
three-pile ; but now I am out of service :

 But shall I go mourn for that, my dear ?
  The pale moon shines by night :
 And when I wander here and there,
  I then do most go right.

 If tinkers may have leave to live,
  And bear the sow-skin budget,

> Then my account I well may give,
> And in the stocks avouch it.

The Scene closes with:

> Jog on, jog on, the foot-path way,
> And merrily hent the stile-a;
> A merry heart goes all the day,
> Your sad tires in a mile-a.

Mr Nicholson has introduced this quatrain into his charming collection of *British Songs for British Boys*, with an additional two verses from what source we cannot say.

Autolycus, the rogue, who does practically all the singing in this Play, is a typical ancient minstrel. Music in the taverns in these merry Elizabethan days was largely provided by strolling musicians or minstrels who were not held in very high esteem. They would enter a tavern uninvited and offer to the convivial company their services, and we gather that they were very difficult to shake off. Towards the end of Elizabeth's reign a law was instituted against these ' sons of the Muses ', and very stern punishment was meted out to them. In Cromwell's time the edict against all minstrels ' wandering abroad ' was greatly strengthened.

We quote at some length from sc. 3 of Act

IV, because these lines contain, as Dr E. W. Naylor says, 'a large quantity of the history of songs in the sixteenth century'.

Enter Servant

Serv. : O Master, if you did but hear the pedlar at the door, you would never dance again after a tabor and pipe; no, the bagpipe could not move you : he sings several tunes faster than you'll tell money ; he utters them as he had eaten ballads and all men's ears grew to his tunes.

Clown : He could never come better; he shall come in. I love a ballad but even too well, if it be doleful matter merrily set down, or a very pleasant thing indeed and sung lamentably.

Serv. : He hath songs for man or woman, of all sizes ; no milliner can so fit his customers with gloves ; he has the prettiest love-songs for maids, etc.

Polixenes : This is a brave fellow.

Clo. : Believe me, thou talkest of an admirable conceited fellow. Has he any unbraided wares ?

Serv. : He hath ribbons of all the colours i' the rainbow ; etc.

Clo. : Prithee, bring him in ; and let him approach singing.

Enter Autolycus, singing

Lawn as white as driven snow;
Cypress black as ere was crow;
Gloves as sweet as damask roses;
Masks for faces and for noses;
Bugle bracelet, necklace amber,
Perfume for a lady's chamber;
Golden quoifs and stomachers,
For my lads to give their dears;
Pins and poking-sticks of steel,
What maids lack from head to heel:
Come buy of me, come; come buy; come buy;
Buy, lads, or else your lasses cry:
Come buy.

Clo. : If I were not in love with Mopsa, thou shouldst take no money from me; but being enthralled as I am, it will also be the bondage of certain ribbons and gloves.

Mop. : I was promised them against the feast; but they come not too late now.

Clo. : What hast here? ballads?

Mop. : Pray now, buy some: I love a ballad in print o' life, for then we are sure they are true.

Aut. : Here's one to a very doleful tune, how a usurer's wife was brought to bed of twenty money-bags at a burthen, and how she longed to eat adders' heads and toads carbonadoed.

Mop. : Is it true, think you?

Aut.: Very true, and but a month old.

Dor.: Bless me from marrying a usurer!

Aut.: Here's the midwife's name to 't, one Mistress Tale-porter, and five or six honest wives that were present. Why should I carry lies abroad?

Mop.: Pray you now, buy it.

Clo.: Come on, lay it by: and let's first see moe ballads; we'll buy the other things anon.

Aut.: Here's another ballad of a fish, that appeared upon the coast, on Wednesday the fourscore of April, forty thousand fathom above water, and sang this ballad against the hard hearts of maids : it was thought she was a woman, and was turned into a cold fish, for she would not exchange flesh with one that loved her: the ballad is very pitiful and as true.

Mop.: Let's have some merry ones.

Aut.: Why, this is a merry one and goes to the tune of 'Two Maids Wooing a Man': there's scarce a maid westward but she sings it; 'tis in request, I can tell you.

Mop.: We can both sing it: if thou'lt bear part, thou shalt hear.

And then we have a three-part Catch as follows :

    A.: Get you hence, for I must go
        Where it fits not you to know,

D.: Whither? *M.:* O, Whither? *D.:* Whither?
M.: It becomes thy oath full well,
　　Thou to me thy secrets tell.
D.: Me too, let me go thither.
M.: Or thou goest to the grange or mill:
D.: If to either, thou dost ill.
A.: Neither. *D.:* What, neither? *A.:* Neither.
D.: Thou hast sworn my love to be;
M.: Thou hast sworn it more to me;
　　Then whither goest? say, whither?　·

Clo.: We'll have this song out anon by ourselves: my father and the gentlemen are in sad
talk, and we'll not trouble them. Come, bring
away thy pack after me. Wenches, I'll buy
for you both. Pedlar, let's have the first choice.
Follow me, girls. (*Exit with Dorcas and Mopsa*)
　Aut.: And you shall pay well for 'em　(*Fol-
　　　　　　　　　　　　　　　　lows singing*)

　　Will you buy any tape,
　　Or lace for your cape,
My dainty duck, my dear-a?
　　Any silk, any thread,　.
　　Any toys for your head,
Of the new'st, and finest, finest wear-a?
　　Come to the pedlar;
　　Money's a medler,
That doth utter all men's ware-a.　　(*Exit*)

A Midsummer Night's Dream

The idea of a ' dream-drama' was perhaps suggested to the mind of Shakespeare by Lyly's *Prologue to his Woman in the Moon*, written some years before *Midsummer Night's Dream :*

Remember all is but a poet's dream,
The first he had in Phoebus' holy bower
But not the last, unless the first displease.

In employing the ' Dream ' as a piece of poetical machinery the Bard of Avon of course links himself to poetical predecessors of a very early period. The conventional allegories of the Medieval Age knew no other medium than that made familiar to them by their favourite ' Romaunt ', a device derived by Lorrie from the quaint Dream-book to which Chaucer often refers— *Scipionis Somnium*, by 'an author hight Macrobes'.

God turn us every dream to good.

The ideas and language of the Elf-world are marvellously imagined and supported in this Play, and the use assigned to Music is happy and fertile to a degree. The style is calculated to arouse in the mind innumerable splendid images or visions peculiar to fairyland. ' Nothing causes us to fall from the ideal world in which the poet conducts us '. The whole Play is ' fanciful, dazzling, ideal and enchanting, a poem indeed, a glorious Lyric of great beauty and buoyancy. As Taine says, 'Love is still the theme; of all sentiments, is it not the greatest fancy-weaver?'

'But we have not here for language the charming tittle-tattle of Rosalind; it is glaring like the season of the year. It does not brim over in slight conversation, in supple and skipping prose; it breaks forth into long rhyming odes, dressed in magnificent metaphors, sustained by impassioned accents, such as a warm night, odorous and star-spangled, inspires in a poet who loves'.

In Act II, sc. 2, Titania calls for 'a roundel and a fairy song'. This appears to be the only occasion on which Shakespeare uses the word 'roundel'. It doubtless means a quick, gay 'dance in a ring' to a lively song and tune.

Titania: Sing me now asleep;
Then to your offices, and let me rest.

Song

First Fairy: You spotted snakes with double
 tongue,
Thorny hedgehogs, be not seen;
Newt and blind-worms, do no wrong,
 Come not near our fairy queen.

Chorus

 Philomel, with melody,
 Sing in our sweet lullaby;

Lulla, lulla, lullaby, lulla, lulla, lullaby :
    Never harm,
    Nor spell, nor charm,
    Come to our lovely lady nigh ;
    So, good night, with lullaby.
First Fairy : Weaving spiders, come not here ;
Hence, you long-legg'd spinners, hence !
Beetles black, approach not near ;
    Worm nor snail, do no offence.

Chorus

    Philomel, with melody, etc.
Sec. Fairy : Hence, away ! now all is well :
One aloof stand sentinel.

    (*Exeunt Fairies.   Titania sleeps*)

In Act III, sc. 1 we have a regular ornithological catalogue in the song which Bottom, the Weaver, sings to show he is not ' afeard '.

    The ousel-cock so black of hue,
      With orange-tawny bill,
    The throstle with his note so true,
      The wren with little quill.
    The finch, the sparrow, and the lark,
      The plain-song cuckoo gray,
    Whose note full many a man doth mark,
      And dares not answer nay :
For, indeed, who would set his wit to so foolish a

bird ? who would give a bird the lie, though he cry 'cuckoo' never so ?

In Act IV, sc. I we are introduced to Rural music indeed.

Titania : What, wilt thou hear some music, my sweet love ?
Bottom : I have a reasonable good ear in music. Let's have the tongs and the bones.

Poker and tongs, cleavers and marrow-bones, salt-box, etc. were some of the old national instruments of music in these Islands.

Oberon, King of the Fairies, asks Titania to call for 'music, such as charmeth sleep'; and in the passage which follows, he refers to music and dancing.

Oberon : Sound, music ! Come, my queen, take hands with me,
And rock the ground wheron these sleepers be.
Now thou and I are new in amity,
And will to-morrow midnight solemnly
Dance in Duke Theseus' house triumphantly,
And bless it to all fair prosperity ;
There shall the pair of faithful lovers be
Wedded, with Theseus, all in jollity.
Puck : Fairy king, attend, and mark:
I do hear the morning lark.

Oberon : Then, my queen, in silence sad,
Trip we after night's shade :
We the globe can compass soon,
Swifter than the wandering moon.
  Titania : Come, my lord ; and in our flight,
Tell me how it came this night,
That I sleeping here was found
With these mortals on the ground.
            (*Exeunt. Horns winded within*)

  In Act V, sc. 1 we meet with a very popular
amusement of the time which is here referred
to as an ' abridgment '. Theseus asks :

  What abridgment have you for this evening ?
  What masque ? what music ? How shall we
      beguile
  The lazy time, if not with some delight ?

  To which the Master of the revels makes reply :

  There is a brief how many sports are ripe :
  Make choice of which your highness will see first.
            (*Giving a paper*)
  Theseus (reads) : The battle with the Centaurs,
      to be sung
  By an Athenian eunuch to the harp.
  We'll none of that : that have I told my love,
  In glory of my kinsman Hercules.   ˏ
  (*Reads*) The riot of the tipsy Bacchanals,
  Tearing the Thracian singer in their rage.

That is an old device ; and it was play'd
When I from Thebes came last a conqueror.

Theseus finally selects a play or masque for
their entertainment. The Masque was a very
popular form of amusement in those days. It
consisted of a Public Procession in which the
characters who were to play rode in decorated
cars, ' accompanied by hobby horses, tumblers,
and open air music '.

The songs referred to by Oberon and Titania
respectively have no doubt been lost.

> *Oberon :* Through the house give glimmering
>   light,
> By the dead and drowsy fire :
> Every elf and fairy sprite
>   Hop as light as bird from brier ;
> And this ditty, after me,
> Sing, and dance it trippingly.
> *Titania :* First, rehearse your song by rote,
> To each word a warbling note :
> Hand in hand, with fairy grace,
> Will we sing, and bless this place.
>   (*Song and dance*)

MUCH ADO ABOUT
NOTHING
THE MERCHANT OF
VENICE
TWO GENTLEMEN
OF VERONA

CHAPTER V

Shakespeare, on whose forehead climb
The crowns o' the world : O eyes sublime,
With tears and laughter for all time !
                              E. B. Browning

MUCH ADO ABOUT NOTHING

THIS Play is a mixture of tragedy and comedy,
and it has been regarded by authorities
like Gollancz and others as the culminating point
of Shakespeare's second period of activity, the
period to which *As You Like It*, *The Merry
Wives*, and *Twelfth Night* belong.

There are a number of allusions to Music,
and many to Dancing in this Play. When
Leonato says to his niece Beatrice, ' Daughter,
remember what I told you : if the prince do
solicit you in that kind, you know your answer '
(Act II, sc. 1), she makes the facetious and finely
cynical reply :

For, hear me, Hero : wooing, wedding, and
repenting, is as a Scotch jig, a measure, and a
cinque-pace : the first suit is hot and hasty, like a

Scotch jig, and full as fantastical ; the wedding, mannerly-modest, as a measure, full of state and ancientry ; and then comes repentance, and, with his bad legs, falls into the cinque-pace faster and faster, till he sink into his grave.

Here several dances are mentioned at one and the same time, as if to give prominence to their individual peculiarities. The Scotch Jig (from German *Geige*=*fiddle*) was a 'round dance' for a number of people, and was characterized by its wild impetuosity. The Measure was staid and formal, and elegant, 'not unlike in its motions to the grace of the Minuet'. The Cinque-pace (or Sinkapace) was the name of the original Galliard—so says Praetorius—a Galliard had five steps, and was therefore called Cinque Pas. The syncopation of the 'cinque-pace' was very quaint and uncertain, so that Beatrice's connexion of it with the tottering and uncertain steps of old age was strangely apt.

We might point out, by the way, how the conversation of the Shakespearean period is 'a masquerade of ideas'. Nothing is stated in a simple style, as we should state it to-day. They seem to love to heap together far-fetched and subtle things, composed with difficulty, and past the wit of man sometimes to understand.

There is much sparkling metaphor in this Play, extraordinary, and to the modern ear over-refined. | It has been urged that much of the ' poetical, sparkling, unreasoning charming wit ' of the time was more akin to music than to literature, a sort of outspoken and wide-awake dream. This is specially noticeable in *Much Ado About Nothing* where thought is changed almost to Caricature. Take as an example some of Benedick's talk on the treatment which had been meted out to him by the Lady Beatrice. ' O, she misused me past the endurance of a block! an oak with but one green leaf on it would have answered her ; my very visor began to assume life and scold with her. She told me . . . that I was duller than a great thaw. . . . She speaks poniards, and every word stabs ; if her breath were as terrible as her terminations, there were no living near her ; she would infect to the north star '. (Act II, sc. 1)

Reference is made to music by Benedick in the very dainty description which he offers of the all-accomplished woman he would ever be inclined to wed. ' Rich she shall be, that's certain ; wise, or I'll none ; virtuous, or I'll never cheapen her ; fair, or I'll never look on her ; mild, or come not near me ; noble, or not I for an angel ; of good discourse, an excellent musician, and her hair shall be of what colour it please God'. (Act II, sc. 2)

A little later on in the same scene the wholly delightful song, 'Sigh no more ladies', is introduced by several reflections of a sarcastic nature, on music and the affectation of singers.

> *Don. Pedro :* Come, shall we hear this music ?
> *Claudio :* Yea, good my lord. How still the
> evening is,
>
> As hush'd on purpose to grace harmony !

> *Enter Balthasar with Music*

> *D. Pedro :* Come, Balthasar, we'll hear that
> song again.
> *Balth. :* O, good my lord, tax not so bad a
> voice
>
> To slander music any more than once.
>
> *D. Pedro :* It is the witness still of excellency
>
> To put a strange face on his own perfection.
> I pray thee, sing, and let me woo no more.
>
> *Balth. :* Because you talk of wooing, I will
> sing ;
>
> Since many a wooer doth commence his suit
> To her he thinks not worthy, yet he wooes,
> Yet will he swear he loves.
>
> *D. Pedro :* Nay, pray thee, come ;
> Or, if thou wilt hold longer argument,
> Do it in notes.

Balth. : Note this before my notes ;
There's not a note of mine that's worth the
noting.

D. Pedro : Why, these are very crotchets that
he speaks ;
Note, notes, forsooth, and nothing.

(*Air*)

Benedick : Now, divine air ! now is his soul
ravished ! Is it not strange that sheeps' guts
should hale souls out of men's bodies ? Well, a
horn for my money, when all's done.

The Song

Balth. : Sigh no more, ladies, sigh no more,
    Men were deceivers ever,
One foot in sea and one on shore,
    To one thing constant never :
Then sigh not so, but let them go,
    And be you blithe and bonny,
Converting all your sounds of woe
    Into Hey, nonny, nonny.

Sing no more ditties, sing no more,
    Of dumps so dull and heavy ;
The fraud of men was ever so,
    Since summer first was leavy ;
    . Then sigh not so, etc.

D. Pedro : By my troth, a good song.

Balth. : And an ill singer, my lord.

D. Pedro : Ha, no, no, faith ; thou singest well enough for a shift.

Benedick : An he had been a dog that should have howled thus, they would have hanged him ; and I pray God his bad voice bode no mischief. I had as lief have heard the night-raven, come what plague could have come after it.

The sentiment of evening being the most fitting time for Music is voiced by Claudio in the passage we have quoted above, and again in a passage in *The Merchant of Venice* Portia descants to Nerissa on the same topic. I think:

The nightingale, if he should sing by day,
When every goose is cackling, would be thought
No better a musician than the wren.
How many things by season season'd are
To their right praise, and true perfection !

So far as we can gather, the song and epitaph in scene 3 have not been set to music, though they are certainly splendidly adapted to that purpose.

Claudio (*reading out of a scroll*) :
    Done to death by slanderous tongues
        Was the Hero that here lies :
    Death, in guerdon of her wrongs,
        Gives her fame which never dies.

So the life that died with shame
Lives in death with glorious fame.

Hang thou there upon the tomb,
Praising her when I am dumb.

Now, music, sound, and sing your solemn hymn.

Song

Pardon, goddess of the night,
Those that slew thy virgin knight;
For the which, with songs of woe,
Round about her tomb they go.
  Midnight, assist our moan;
  Help us to sigh and groan,
     Heavily, heavily:
  Graves, yawn, and yield your dead,
  Till death be uttered,
     Heavily, heavily.

(Act V, sc. 3)

THE MERCHANT OF VENICE

Taine calls *The Merchant of Venice* one of
Shakespeare's half-dramas. With reference to
it and some others of his plays, he pictures the
Author meeting the readers on the threshold
and telling them, to prevent all misunderstanding,
'Do not take too seriously what you are about
to hear; I am joking. My brain being full of

fancies, desired to make plays of them, and here they are. Palaces, distant landscapes, transparent mists which blot the morning sky with their gray clouds, the red and glorious flames into which the evening sun descends, white cloisters in endless vista through the ambient air, grottos, cottages, the fantastic pageant of all human passions, the mad sport of unlooked-for chances,—this is the medley of forms, colours, sentiments, which I shuffle and mingle before me, a many-tinted skein of glistening silks, a slender arabesque, whose sinuous curves, crossing and confused, bewilder the mind by the whimsical variety of their infinite complications. Don't regard it as a picture. Don't look for a precise composition, harmonious and increasing interest, the skilful management of a well-ordered and congruous plot. Never mind the finis, I am amusing myself on the road. It is not the end of the journey which pleases me, but the journey itself '.

The story of *The Merchant of Venice* is said to have a Buddhist origin; there is certainly much of the glamour and mystic flavour of the East in many of its ideas, and it may well have found its way from India to Europe.

In Act III, sc. 2 we have a hint of the many beautiful and suggestive musical allusions which

are to follow in the latter part of the Play.   Here
Portia is making preparations for Bassanio to
examine the several caskets.

Portia : I am lock'd in one of them :
If you do love me, you will find me out.
Nerissa and the rest, stand all aloof.
Let music sound while he doth make his choice,
Then, if he lose, he makes a swan-like end,
Fading in music ; that the comparison
May stand more proper, my eye shall be the
    stream,
And watery death-bed for him.   He may win
And what is music then ?   Then music is
Even as the flourish when true subjects bow
To a new-crowned monarch ; such it is
As are those dulcet sounds in break of day
That creep into the dreaming bridegroom's ear,
And summon him to marriage.

Then follows a Song while Bassanio comments
on the caskets to himself.

Song

   Tell me where is fancy bred,
   Or in the heart or in the head ?
   How begot, how nourished ?
      Reply, reply.
   It is engender'd in the eyes,

> With gazing fed ; and fancy dies
> In the cradle where it lies.
> Let us all ring fancy's knell ;
> I'll begin it,—Ding, dong, bell.

All : Ding, dong, bell.

With the conclusion of the Fourth Act, Shylock disappears from the scene in order that, as some one has beautifully put it, 'no discord may mar the harmony of the concluding scene'. The passages in Act V are not only celebrated, many of them at least, but those relating to music are beautiful exceedingly. Brandes compares the whole act to 'a moonlit landscape thrilled with music'. Moonshine and music make up the picture. The speeches on Music by Lorenzo and Portia melt into each other even as do well-trained voices in a Part-song. Here we have the 'very poetry of moonlight arranged in antiphonies'.

> *Lorenzo :* The moon shines bright : in such a
>   night as this,
> When the sweet wind did gently kiss the trees
> And they did make no noise, in such a night
> Troilus methinks mounted the Trojan walls,
> And 'sigh'd his soul toward the Grecian tents,
> Where Cressid lay that night.

Lorenzo : How sweet the moonlight sleeps
    upon this bank!
Here will we sit, and let the sounds of music
Creep in our ears : soft stillness and the night
Become the touches of sweet harmony.
Sit, Jessica. Look how the floor of heaven
Is thick inlaid with patines of bright gold :
There's not the smallest orb which thou be-
    hold'st
But in his motion like an angel sings,
Still quiring to the young-eyed cherubins ;
Such harmony is in immortal souls ;
But while this muddy vesture of decay
Doth grossly close it in, we cannot hear it.

Enter Musicians

Come, ho, and wake Diana with a hymn!
With sweetest touches pierce your mistress' ear,
And draw her home with music.   (*Music*)
    Jessica : I am never merry when I hear sweet
    music.
    Lorenzo : The reason is, your spirits are atten-
    tive :
For do but note a wild and wanton herd,
Or race of youthful and unhandled colts,
Fetching mad bounds, bellowing and neighing
    loud,
Which is the hot condition of their blood ;

If they but hear perchance a trumpet sound,
Or any air of music touch their ears,
You shall perceive them make a mutual stand,
Their savage eyes turn'd to a modest gaze
By the sweet power of music : therefore the poet
Did feign that Orpheus drew trees, stones and
    floods ;
Since nought so stockish, hard and full of rage,
But music for the time doth change his nature.

Then follow the notable lines which have given
rise to much lively debate among the com-
mentators of Shakespeare, some holding that they
were written in order to curry favour with
the public of the times, which was supremely
musical; others contending that the sentiment
they inshrine is quite out of keeping with sentiments on music put into the mouths of other
strong characters of the Poet's creation, Othello
for example, and Harry Hotspur. See *Othello*
Act III, sc. 1 and *Henry IV*, Part I :

The man that hath no music in himself,
Nor is not moved with concord of sweet sounds,
Is fit for treasons, stratagems and spoils ;
The motions of his spirit are dull as night
And his affections dark as Erebus :
Let no such man be trusted. Mark the Music.

In our remarks on *Much Ado About Nothing*

we referred to Shakespeare's double reference
to Evening as ' the most fitting frame for Music ',
the kindred sentiment being put in the mouth
of Claudio, and in that of Portia respectively.

Portia : Music ! hark !
Nerissa : It is your music, madam, of the
house.
Portia : Nothing is good, I see, without re-
spect :
Methinks it sounds much sweeter than by day.

etc.

The Play ends on a note of perfect harmony.
Everything is ' reconciled, assuaged, silvered
over, and borne aloft upon the wings of music '.

' The conclusion of *The Merchant of Venice*
brings us to the threshold of a term in Shakespeare's life instinct with high-pitched gaiety
and gladness. In this, his brightest period, he
fervently celebrates strength and wisdom in man,
intellect and wit in women ; and these most
brilliant years of his life are also the most musical.
His poetry, his whole existence, seem now to be
given over to music, to harmony '.

TWO GENTLEMEN OF VERONA

The *Two Gentlemen of Verona* is a very bright,
mirth-provoking comedy, quick with tender

feeling. The love-interest predominates. There are many allusions to matters musical in it.

In the second scene of the First Act a great number of terms then in everyday use in connexion with the Art of Singing are introduced by Lucetta, when she tries, by guile, to bring Proteus's note to the attention of her charming but seemingly ' unwilling ' mistress.

Lucetta : What would your ladyship ?
Julia : Is't near dinner-time ?
Luc. : I would it were ;
That you might kill your stomach on your meat,
And not upon your maid.
Jul. : What is't that you took up so gingerly ?
Luc. : Nothing.
Jul. : Why didst thou stoop then ?
Luc. : To take a paper up that I let fall.
Jul. : And is that paper nothing ?
Luc. : Nothing concerning me.
Jul. : Then let it lie for those that it concerns.
Luc. : Madam, it will not lie where it concerns,
Unless it have a false interpreter.
Jul. : Some love of yours hath writ to you in
rhyme.
Luc. : That I might sing it, madam, to a tune.
Give me a note : your ladyship can set.
Jul. : As little by such toys as may be possible.

Best sing it to the tune of 'Light o' Love'.

Luc. : It is too heavy for so light a tune.

Jul. : Heavy! belike it hath some burden, then ?

Luc. : Ay; and melodious were it, would you sing it.

Jul. : And why not you ?

Luc. : I cannot reach so high.

Jul. : Let's see your song.   How now, minion !

Luc. : Keep tune there still, so you will sing it out :

And yet methinks I do not like this tune.

Jul. : You do not ?

Luc. : No, madam ; it is too sharp.

Jul. : You, minion, are too saucy.

Luc. : Nay, now you are too flat,

And mar the concord with too harsh a descant :

There wanteth but a mean to fill your song.

Jul. : The mean is drown'd with your unruly bass.

Luc. : Indeed, I bid the base for Proteus.

Jul. : This babble shall not henceforth trouble me.

Here is a coil with protestation !

(*Tears the letter*)

Go get you gone, and let the papers lie :
You would be fingering them, to anger me.

G

Luc.: She makes it strange ; but she would be
   best pleased
To be so anger'd with another letter.   (*Exit*)

As Mr Elson says, a whole chapter of musical
comment and explanation might well be devoted to this scene.

The tune 'Light o' Love', mentioned in
above passage, seems to have been a favourite
with Shakespeare.   It is not known what words
were sung to the tune, but the old melody is
still extant, and has been reproduced for us in
Elson's *Shakespeare in Music*, page 100.

In Act III, sc. 2 we have a rather laboured
description of the powers of Poetry and Music in
Proteus's advice on courtship to one of Silvia's
suitors.

Proteus : As much as I can do, I will effect ;
But you, Sir Thurio, are not sharp enough ;
You must lay lime to tangle her desires
By wailful sonnets, whose composed rhymes
Should be full-fraught with serviceable vows.
   Duke : Ay,
Much is the force of heaven-bred poesy.
   Pro. : Say that upon the altar of her beauty
You sacrifice your tears, your sighs, your heart :
Write till your ink be dry, and with your tears

Moist it again; and frame some feeling line
That may discover such integrity:
For Orpheus' lute was strung with poets' sinews;
Whose golden touch could soften steel and stones,
Make tigers tame, and huge leviathans
Forsake unsounded deeps to dance on sands.
After your dire-lamenting elegies,
Visit by night your lady's chamber-window
With some sweet consort; to their instruments
Tune a deploring dump: the night's dead silence
Will well become such sweet-complaining
    grievance.
This, or else nothing, will inherit her.
  Thurio: And thy advice this night I'll put in
    practice.
Therefore, sweet Proteus, my direction-giver,
Let us into the city presently
To sort some gentlemen well skill'd in music.
I have a sonnet that will serve the turn
To give the onset to thy good advice.

The Serenade, duly arranged, takes place in
the following Act (Act V, sc. 2) when Thurio and
his musicians appear outside the Duke's palace,
under Silvia's chamber-window.

  Thurio: Now, gentlemen,
Let's tune, and to it lustily awhile.

*Enter, at a distance, Host, and Julia in boy's
clothes*

Host : Now, my young guest, methinks you're
Allycholly : I pray you, why is it ?

Julia : Marry, mine host, because I cannot be
merry.

Host : Come, we'll have you merry : I'll bring
you where you shall hear music, and see the
gentleman that you asked for.

Julia : But shall I hear him speak ?

Host : Ay, that you shall.

Julia : That will be music.   (*Music plays*)

Host : Hark, hark !

Julia : Is he among these ?

Host : Ay : but, peace ! let's hear 'em.

Then we have the delightful song which has
been set to a score of different tunes—'Who is
Silvia ? ' :

Who is Silvia ?   what is she,
   That all our swains commend her ?
Holy, fair, and wise is she ;
   The heaven such grace did lend her,
That she might admired be.

Is she kind as she is fair ?
   For beauty lives with kindness.

Love doth to her eyes repair,
  To help him of his blindness,
And, being help'd, inhabits there.

Then to Silvia let us sing,
  That Silvia is excelling;
She excels each mortal thing
  Upon the dull earth dwelling:
To her ·let us garlands bring.

There follows a passage full of most entertaining quibbles on musical terms.

Host: How now! are you sadder than you were before?
How do you, man? the music likes you not.
Julia: You mistake; the musician likes me not.
Host: Why, my pretty youth?
Julia: He plays false, father.
Host: How? out of tune on the strings?
Julia: Not so, but yet so false that he grieves my very heartstrings.
Host: You have a quick ear.
Julia: Ay, I would I were deaf; it makes me have a slow heart.
Host: I perceive you delight not in music.
Julia: Not a whit, when it jars so.
Host: Hark, what fine change is in the music!

Julia: Ay, that change is the spite.

Host: You would have them always play but one thing?

Julia: I would always have one play but one thing.

But, host, doth this Sir Proteus that we talk on
Often resort unto this gentlewoman?

Host: I tell you what Launce, his man, told me,—he loved her out of all nick.

Julia: Where is Launce?

Host: Gone to seek his dog; which to-morrow, by his master's command, he must carry for a present to his lady.

Julia: Peace! stand aside: the company parts.

Proteus: Sir Thurio, fear not you: I will so plead,

That you shall say my cunning drift excels.

Thurio: Where meet we?

Proteus: At Saint Gregory's well.

Thurio: Farewell.

(*Exeunt Thu. and Musicians*)

CHAPTER VI

I close your Marlowe's page, my Shakespeare's ope,
 How welcome—after gong and cymbal's din—
The continuity, the long slow slope
 And vast curves of the gradual violin.
                              William Watson.

MEASURE FOR MEASURE

THERE is little music, and but few musical allusions in this Play. Not, indeed, until we arrive at Act IV do we come on anything musical. In the first scene of this act, a song from his own *Passionate Pilgrim* is sung to Mariana by a boy, as follows :

Take, O, take those lips away,
  That so sweetly were forsworn ;
And those eyes, the break of day,
  Lights that do mislead the morn :
But my kisses bring again, bring again ;
Seals of love, but seal'd in vain, seal'd in vain.

To this song belongs the honour of the most copious setting of any of Shakespeare's lyrics—

more than thirty different settings are known to exist.

> *Mariana :* Break off thy song, and haste thee
>   quick away :
> Here comes a man of comfort, whose advice
> Hath often still'd my brawling discontent.
>
> (Exit boy)

The Duke, disguised as a friar, here enters.

> *Mar. :* I cry you mercy, sir ; and well could
>   wish
> You had not found me here so musical :
> Let me excuse me, and believe me so,
> My mirth it much displeased, but pleased my
>   woe.
> *Duke :* 'Tis good ; though music oft hath such
>   a charm
> To make bad good, and good provoke to harm.

This dictum of the Duke's is very curious, especially in face of what is said in other of the Dramas as to the innocuous effect of music. It contains a charge somewhat difficult, we should think, to prove. But the whole point here raised of the ethical effect of music is absorbingly interesting, and well worthy of much more earnest attention than it has yet received. Such an Art as Music, which touches so directly and powerfully upon the whole gamut of the emotional life of man, must necessarily have enormous force as a means of culture, and ethical upbuilding. Just what that influence may be, or how far a musical education may effect character, is still a question that is open for serious discussion. When charges are made against artists and musicians that many of them are morally weak, and even depraved, such charges prove nothing from an ethical standpoint; all they prove is the 'fact that artistic genius does not always imply a corresponding degree of ethical attainment'. We heartily agree with Mr H. H. Britan when he contends that the emotional character of music prevents it from imparting to the hearer a principle or a definite conclusion. 'By nature it is ill-fitted to be didactic. As an art it is least able to present to the hearer a definite train of logical thought'. An old writer says, 'Music may be applied to licentious poetry; but the poetry then corrupts the music, not the music the poetry'.

True, music may often have regulated the movements of a lascivious dance, but such an air, heard, say, for the first time, without any accompanying words or movement, would certainly convey no impure thought or idea to an innocent imagination. Montesquieu's assertion is right,

we think, ' Music is the only one of all the arts,
which does not corrupt the mind '. Or, to
put it in other words, ' Music in itself, however
sensuous, is neither moral nor immoral '. We
can only speak of music as having an ethical value
when it has been assimilated, so to speak, and
become an integral part of character, or ' when we
consider it as a stimulus that excites passions
that lead to immoral practices '.

The conclusion we may come to, in estimating
the value of the Duke's dictum, as above, is that
' the highest development, even from the moral
point of view, demands just that sort of cultiva-
tion of the emotional nature which music in its
better forms promotes '.

An able and original article on Music and
Morality, and which is apropos of above remarks,
appeared in the *International Journal of Ethics*
in October, 1904 (Vol. XV), over the signature
Halbert H. Britan.

ALL'S WELL THAT ENDS WELL

Brandes, Gollancz, and others are inclined to
the view that this Play originally bore the title
of *Love's Labour's Won*, and was a counterpart to
the Comedy of *Love's Labour's Lost*. It contains
many passages which quite evidently belong

to an earlier version, rhymed letters in sonnet form, and other details which, in the eyes of an expert, make it correspond · with the style of the before-mentioned play, *Love's Labour's Lost.*

With the exception, perhaps, of the mention of Flourish in several scenes, and reference to the Canary and Morris dances, together with the Clown's song in Act I, sc. 3 there is no allusion to Music in this interesting and exciting comedy. The song which the Clown sings, and the speeches to which it gives rise, with all the youthful whimsicality attached, belong, without much doubt, to the early creative period of the Poet.

Clown : A prophet I, madam ; and I speak the
    truth the next way :
For I the ballad will repeat,
    Which men full true shall find ;
Your marriage comes by destiny,
    Your cuckoo sings by kind.
Count : Get you gone, sir ; I'll talk with you more anon.
Steward : May it please you, madam, that he bid Helen come to you : of her I am to speak.
Count : Sirrah, tell my gentlewoman I would speak with her ; Helen I mean.
Clown : Was this fair face the cause, quoth he,

Why the Grecians sacked Troy?
Fond done, done fond,
    Was this King Priam's joy?
With that she sighed as she stood,
With that she sighed as she stood,
    And gave this sentence then;
Among nine bad if one be good,
Among nine bad if one be good,
    There's yet one good in ten.

Count : What, one good in ten? You corrupt
the song, sirrah.

Clown : One good woman in ten, madam;
which is a purifying of the song: would God
would serve the world so all the year! we'd find
no fault with the tithe-woman, if I were the
parson: one in ten quoth 'a! an we might
have a good woman born but one every blazing
star, or at an earthquake, 'twould mend the
lottery well: a man may draw his heart out, ere
a' pluck one.   (Act I, sc. 3)

THE MERRY WIVES OF WINDSOR

As *King John* is characterized by an absence of
prose in its composition, *The Merry Wives of
Windsor* is the only play of Shakespeare written
almost entirely in prose. It belongs to the
period when the Author's genius was at its

freest and brightest, and when his laughter was 'clear and musical'.   Dowden accepts the tradition that the Play was written at the command of Queen Elizabeth, 'who in her lust for gross mirth, required the poet to expose his Falstaff to ridicule, by exhibiting him, the most delightful of egoists, in love'.   Though the Play is consistently farcical, there is much real poetry in it, and it gives us a faithful picture, no doubt, of the middle-class life of his day.

In Act III, sc. 1 we have the song by Parson Evans 'To Shallow Rivers'.   While Evans, in a state of nervous tension, is waiting for the French physician Caius, he begins to sing :

> To shallow rivers, to whose falls
> Melodious birds sing madrigals ;
> There will we make our peds of roses,
> And a thousand fragrant posies.
> To shallow—

Mercy on me !   I have a great dispositions to cry.   (*Sings*)

> Melodious birds sing madrigals—
> When as I sat in Pabylon—
> And a thousand vagram posies.
> To shallow, etc.

In his nervous condition, the Parson muddles

up the words of the song with lines from a metrical version of the 137th Psalm, and at last breaks down hopelessly.

In the last scene of all, while the fairies pinch Falstaff they sing the scornful rhyme (Act V sc. 5):

Fie on sinful fantasy!
Fie on lust and luxury!
Lust is but a bloody fire,
Kindled with unchaste desire,
Fed in heart, whose flames aspire,
As thoughts do blow them, higher and higher.
Pinch him, fairies, mutually;
Pinch him for his villany;
Pinch him, and burn him, and turn him about,
Till candles, and starlight, and moonshine be out.

THE TAMING OF THE SHREW

As in the case of *Twelfth Night*, there is much musical metaphor in *The Taming of The Shrew*. Many fragments of old ballads are referred to in this Play, though, as Warburton says, ' Shakespeare seemed to bear the ballad-makers a very particular grudge, and often ridicules them with exquisite humour '.

The first reference to singing is in Act I, sc. 2, when Petruchio bullies his servant Grumio.

Before Hortensio's House

Pet. : Here, sirrah Grumio ; knock, I say.
Grum. : Knock, sir ! whom should I knock ?
is there any man has rebused your worship ?

Grum. : My master is grown quarrelsome.
  I should knock you first,
And then I know after who comes by the worst.
Pet. : Will it not be ?
Faith, sirrah, an you'll not knock, I'll ring it ;
I'll try how you can sol, fa, and sing it.

(*He wrings him by the ears*)

Gru. : Help, masters, help ! my master is mad.
Pet. : Now, knock when I bid you, sirrah
  villain.

In the beginning of Act II we are treated to
the inimitable picture of what the poor Music-
master Hortensio has to put up with at the hands
of his shrewish and lively pupil Katharine.

Re-enter Hortensio, with his head broke

Bap. : Now, now, my friend ! why dost thou
  look so pale ?
Hor. : For fear, I promise you, if I look pale.
Bap. : What, will my daughter prove a good
  musician ?

H

Hor. : I think she'll sooner prove a soldier :
Iron may hold with her, but never lutes.

    Bap. : Why, then thou canst not break her
       to the lute ?

    Hor. : Why, no ; for she hath broke the lute to
       me.

I did but tell her she mistook her frets,
And bow'd her hand to teach her fingering ;
When, with a most impatient devilish spirit,
' Frets, call you these ? ' quoth she ; ' I'll fume
    with them ' :
And, with that word, she struck me on the head,
And through the instrument my pate made
    way ;
And there I stood amazed for a while,
As on a pillory, looking through the lute ;
While she did call me rascal fiddler
And twangling Jack ; with twenty such vile terms
As had she studied to misuse me so.

In Act III, sc. 1 we have more delightful
musical badinage between the sham musical and
classical tutors, Hortensio and Lucentio. They
quarrel as to who is to be the first to give a lesson.

    Luc : Fiddler, forbear ; you grow too forward,
       sir :

    Hor. : But, wrangling pedant, this is
The patroness of heavenly harmony :

Then give me leave to have prerogative ;
And when in music we have spent an hour,
Your lecture shall have leisure for as much.

    Luc. : Preposterous ass, that never read so far
To know the cause why music was ordain'd !
Was it not to refresh the mind of man
After his studies or his usual pain ?
Then give me leave to read philosophy,
And while I pause, serve in your harmony.

    Hor. : Sirrah, I will not bear these braves of
    thine.

    Then follows Lucentio's novel Latin lesson,
and Hortensio's music lesson which contains some
delicate allusions to the tuning of the Lute.

    There are two references in this Play to the
importance which was then attached to music
as part of a ' liberal education '. (Act I, sc. 1,
line 90, and Act 1, sc. 2, line 172)

COMEDY OF ERRORS

    This seems to be one of the very few plays in
which music bears not the slightest part. This
is all the more strange when we consider the
opportunities for introducing music of one kind
or another, with all the mad jesting, balls, and
sport that make up the Comedy.

The Sonnets

The musical references in the sonnets are few and far between, and are almost entirely of a technical character. See *Sonnets* VIII and CXXVIII.

The Rape of Lucrece

The remarkable passage in this poem, from a musical point of view, is that beginning at line 1121. In four consecutive stanzas, the Poet draws upon Music for all kinds of similes, and these are marvellously apt and telling.

'You mocking birds', quoth she, 'your tunes
    entomb
Within your hollow-swelling feather'd breasts,
And in my hearing be you mute and dumb :
My restless discord loves no stops nor rests ;
A woful hostess brooks not merry guests :
    Relish your nimble notes to pleasing ears ;
    Distress likes dumps when time is kept with tears

'Come Philomel, that sing'st of ravishment,
Make thy sad grove in my dishevell'd hair :
As the dank earth weeps at thy languishment,
So I at each sad strain will strain a tear,
And with deep groans the diapason bear ;
    For burden-wise I'll hum on Tarquin still,
    While thou on Tereus descant'st better skill.

' And whiles against a thorn thou bear'st thy
　　part,
To keep thy sharp woes waking, wretched I,
To imitate thee well, against my heart
Will fix a sharp knife, to affright my eye;
Who, if it wink, shall thereon fall and die.
　　These means, as frets upon an instrument,
　　Shall tune our heart-strings to true languish-
　　　ment.

' And for, poor bird, thou sing'st not in the day,
As shaming any eye should thee behold,
Some dark deep desert, seated from the way,
That knows not parching heat nor freezing cold,
Will we find out; and there we will unfold
　　To creatures stern sad tunes, to change their
　　　kinds :
　　Since men prove beasts, let beasts bear gentle
　　　minds '.

VENUS AND ADONIS

The musical allusions in this poem are few and
somewhat fragmentary.

At line 835 Venus

　　　　　　　　　begins a wailing note,
And sings extemporally a woful ditty;
How love makes young men thrall, and old men
　　dote;

How love is wise in folly, foolish-witty :
  Her heavy anthem still concludes in woe,
  And still the choir of echoes answer so.

Her song was tedious, and outwore the night,
For lovers' hours are long, though seeming short.

A musical note is referred to in line 700.
' Alarum ' is here used to denote the sound made
by the dogs in pursuit of the wild boar. The term
is used frequently in Shakespeare, but it has
different meanings, sometimes indicating the
sound of ' drums ' and at other times the sound
of ' trumpets '.

RICHARD II
OTHELLO
KING JOHN
HENRY IV
HENRY V
HENRY VI
HENRY VIII
JULIUS CÆSAR
TIMON OF ATHENS
CORIOLANUS
KING LEAR

CHAPTER VII

When great poets sing,
Into the night new constellations spring,
With music in the air that dulls the craft
Of rhetoric. So when Shakespeare sang or laughed,
The world with long, sweet Alpine echoes thrilled
Voiceless to scholars' tongues no muse had filled
With melody divine.

C. P. Chance.

RICHARD II

THIS tragedy is of great interest to all students of Shakespeare, since it is probably the Poet's first attempt at independent treatment of a historical theme. It has never taken any great hold on the Stage ; the action is too exclusively political, and there is a great lack of female character in it. The character of the Queen, the sole female character, indeed, which is portrayed, is quite unhistorical, and must have been invented by Shakespeare for the sake of introducing some female interest and colour into his play.

There are a few very beautiful musical references in this Play. In the opening scene of the

Second Act, John of Gaunt, who is ill and waiting for a visit from his King, thus speaks to the Duke of York:

> *Gaunt:* Will the king come, that I may breathe my last
> In wholesome counsel to his unstaid youth?
> *York:* Vex not yourself, nor strive not with your breath;
> For all in vain comes counsel to his ear.
> *Gaunt:* O, but they say the tongues of dying men
> Enforce attention like deep harmony:
> Where words are scarce, they are seldom spent in vain,
> For they breathe truth that breathe their words in pain.
> He that no more must say is listen'd more
> Than they whom youth and ease have taught to glose;
> More are men's ends mark'd than their lives before:
> The setting sun, and music at the close,
> As the last taste of sweets, is sweetest last,
> Writ in remembrance more than things long past.

When word is brought the King that Gaunt is dead, in the subtle remark of Northumberland's, 'My liege, old Gaunt commends him to your

majesty', and the King replies, 'What says
he ? ', Northumberland makes answer in the
clever musical metaphor :

> Nay, nothing ; all is said :
> His tongue is now a stringless instrument :
> Words, life and all, old Lancaster hath spent.

In Act V, sc. 5 we have an exquisite soliloquy
on Music from the lips of Richard, as he lies a
prisoner in Pomfret Castle.

> Music do I hear ?
> Ha, ha ! keep time : how sour sweet music is
> When time is broke and no proportion kept !
> So is it in the music of men's lives.
> And here have I the daintiness of ear
> To check time broke in a disorder'd string ;
> But for the concord of my state and time
> Had not an ear to hear my true time broke.
> I wasted time, and now doth time waste me ;
> For now hath time made me his numbering clock :
> My thoughts are minutes ; and with sighs they jar
> Their watches on unto mine eyes, the outward
>   watch,
> Whereto my finger, like a dial's point,
> Is pointing still, in cleansing them from tears.
> Now sir, the sound that tells what hour it is
> Are clamorous groans, which strike upon my
>   heart,

Which is the bell : so sighs and tears and groans
Show minutes, times, and hours : but my time
Runs posting on in Bolingbroke's proud joy,
While I stand fooling here, his Jack o' the clock.
This music mads me ; let it sound no more ;
For though it have holp madmen to their wits,
In me it seems it will make wise men mad.
Yet blessing on his heart that gives it me !
For 'tis a sign of love ; and love to Richard
Is a strange brooch in this all-hating world.

OTHELLO

In Act II, sc. 3 we have two songs from Iago
when he is simulating friendship with Cassio.

Iago : Some wine, ho !
(*Sings*) And let me the canakin clink, clink ;
   And let me the canakin clink :
    A soldier's a man ;
    A life's but a span ;
   Why, then, let a soldier drink.
Some wine, boys !

Cassio : 'Fore God, an excellent song.

Iago : I learned it in England, where indeed
they are most potent in potting : your Dane,
your German, and your swag-bellied Hollander,
Drink, ho ! are nothing to your English.

Cassio : Is your Englishman so expert in his
drinking ?

Iago : Why, he drinks you, with facility, your Dane dead drunk ; he sweats not to overthrow your Almain ; he gives your Hollander a vomit, ere the next pottle can be filled.

Cassio : To the health of our general !

Mon. : I am for it, lieutenant, and I'll do you justice.

Iago : O sweet England.

(*Sings*) King Stephen was a worthy peer
   His breeches cost him but a crown ;
  He held them sixpence all too dear,
   With that he call'd the tailor lown.

He was a wight of high renown,
 And thou art but of low degree :
'Tis pride that pulls the country down ;
 Then take thine auld cloak about thee.

Some wine, ho !

In Act IV. sc. 3 we have the well-known, tragic song of Desdemona's. The ' willow ' which is mentioned in the song was emblematic of unhappy love, and the idea had been used by Spenser in his *Faerie Queene*. ' The willow, worne of forlorne Paramours '. Desdemona, possessed with a presentiment of coming tragedy, says to Emilia :

My mother had a maid call'd Barbara :
She was in love ; and he she loved proved mad

And did forsake her : she had a song of ' willow ; '
An old thing 'twas, but it express'd her fortune,
And she died singing it : that song to-night
Will not go from my mind ; I have much to do
But to go hang my head all on one side
And sing it like poor Barbara.   Prithee, dispatch.

    Emil.   Shall I go fetch your night-gown ?

    Des. : No, unpin me here.

This Lodovico is a proper man.

    Emil. : A very handsome man.

    Des. : He speaks well.

    Emil. I know a lady in Venice would have
walked barefoot to Palestine for a touch of his
nether lip.

    Des. : (*singing*) The poor soul sat sighing by a
        sycamore tree,
      Sing all a green willow ;
    Her hand on her bosom, her head on her knee,
      Sing willow, willow, willow :
    The fresh streams ran by her, and murmur'd
        her moans ;
      Sing willow, willow, willow :
    Her salt tears fell from her, and soften'd the
        stones :—

Lay by these :—

    (*singing*) Sing willow, willow, willow : [1]

Prithee, hie thee ; he'll come anon :—

   [1] The traditional setting of this is given on page 176.

(*singing*) Sing all a green willow must be
    my garland
Let nobody blame him; his scorn I ap-
    prove,—
Nay, that's not next. Hark! who is't that
    knocks ?
Emil. : It's the wind.
Des. : (*singing*) I call'd my love false love;
    but what said he then ?
    Sing willow, willow, willow.
If I court moe women, you'll couch with
    moe men.
So get thee gone ; good night.   Mine eyes do itch :
Doth that bode weeping ?

There is a clever and most effective metaphor
in Act II, sc. 1 taken from the tuning and un-
tuning of a musical instrument. Desdemona
says to Othello that their loves and comforts
should increase even as their days do grow.   To
which Othello answers ' Amen to that, sweet
powers ! '

I cannot speak enough of this content ;
It stops me here ; it is too much of joy :
And this, and this, the greatest discords be,
                       (*kissing her*)
That e'er our hearts shall make !

Iago : (*aside*) O, you are well tuned now!
But I'll set down the pegs that make this music,
As honest as I am.

Every musician will realize the wonderful
aptness of the allusion—how discord is brought
about by tampering with the tuning-pins of an
instrument.

KING JOHN

Belonging, in all likelihood to the same group
of Plays as *Richard II* and *Richard III*, like
them, *King John* is characterized by an absence
of prose in its composition. It is almost wholly
lacking in any musical allusion. The dying
King had attempted to sing, and Prince Henry
comments on the fact in the striking and beautiful
lines

Pembroke :   He is more patient
Than when you left him ; even now he sung.
   Prince Henry : O vanity of sickness! fierce
      extremes
In their continuance will not feel themselves
'Tis strange that death should sing.
I am the cygnet to this pale faint swan,
Who chants a doleful hymn to his own death,
And from the organ-pipe of frailty sings
His soul and body to their lasting rest.

HENRY IV, PART I, AND PART II

There is much musical allusion in this Play, and among all the historical dramas, this seems to have possessed peculiar attraction for librettists and composers. Tavern songs are provided by Justice Silence in a Gloucestershire orchard where a number of 'worthies' have met, and these ditties are thoroughly representative of the Bacchanalian music of these rough and ready times. See Part II, Act V, sc. 3.

Silence : Do nothing but eat, and make good
    cheer,   *(singing)*
And praise God for the merry year ;
When flesh is cheap and females dear ;
And lusty lads roam here and there.
    So merrily.
And ever among so merrily.

Shallow : Be merry, Master Bardolph ; and, my little soldier there, be merry.

Silence : Be merry, be merry, my wife has all ;
                                     (singing)
For women are shrews, both short and tall :
'Tis merry in hall when beards wag all,
And welcome merry Shrove-tide.
Be merry, be merry.

Fal. : I did not think Master Silence had been a man of this mettle.

I

Sil. : Who, I ? I have been merry twice and once ere now.

Davy (to Bardolph) : A cup of wine, sir ?

Sil. : A cup of wine that's brisk and fine,
                                          (*singing*)
And drink unto the leman mine;
And a merry heart lives long-a.

Fal. : Well said, Master Silence.

Sil. : And we shall be merry, now comes in the weet o' the night.

Fal. : Health and long life to you, Master Silence.

Sil. : Fill the cup, and let it come ; (*singing*)
I'll pledge you a mile to the bottom.

Fal.   Why, now you have done me right.
     (*To Silence, seeing him take off a bumper*)
Sil. :   Do me right,
                And club me knight.
                    Samingo.

Is't not so ?

There is an allusion to the bagpipe in the first part of this play which has given rise to some discussion among critics. In Act I, sc. 2 Falstaff says to Prince Hal that he is as melancholy as the ' drone of a Lincolnshire bagpipe '.

Lampooning by means of ballads was fairly common in Shakespeare's day, and in these plays

Falstaff threatens his tormentors with that form of punishment.

Fal. : Go hang thyself in thine own heir-apparent garters ! . . . If I be ta'en, I'll peach for this. An I have not ballads made on you all and sung to filthy tunes, let a cup of sack be my poison : when a jest is so forward, and afoot too ! I hate it.

Henry IV, Part I, Act II, sc. 2

Fal. : or, by the Lord, I will have it in a particular ballad else, with mine own picture on the top on't, Colevile kissing my feet : etc.

Henry IV, Part II, Act IV, sc. 3

In the same play, Hotspur refers contemptu-ously to those 'metre ballad-mongers', and vows that he had rather 'be a kitten and cry mew' than be one of them. (Part I, Act III, sc. 1) And on one occasion the hot-tempered Prince broke Falstaff's head because he had compared his father to a 'singing-man of Windsor'. (Part II, Act II, sc. 1)

HENRY V

The musical terms and allusions employed in this fine heroic Lyric are very numerous, but they are entirely of a technical character, dealing with Instrumental notes, Dances, Counterpoint, etc.

The prologue to each Act consists of a Chorus, and these five choruses, together with the Epilogue, constitute one glorious patriotic pæan to England—to a united and powerful Great Britain.

Act I, sc. 2 : Reference to Counterpoint.

Act II, sc. 4 : Whitsun Morris-dance.

Act III, sc. 2 : Reference to lute-case.

Act III, sc. 2 : Reference to Plain-song.

Act IV, sc. 2 : The 'Tucket' sound. This seems to be the only occasion on which the word is used in the text, though it is used repeatedly as a stage-direction.

Act V, sc. 2 : The King puns on 'broken music'.

Henry VI, Parts I, II, and III

With the exception of several technical musical terms there is nothing directly musical in any of the Parts of this Play.

Henry VIII

The most interesting item in *Henry VIII* to musical readers of the Play is the charming and justly popular song, 'Orpheus with his Lute'.

This was sung to the accompaniment of the lute,
at the request of Queen Katharine.   (Act I, sc. 1)

> Orpheus with his lute made trees,
> And the mountain tops that freeze,
> > Bow themselves when he did sing :
> To his music plants and flowers
> Ever sprung, as sun and showers
> > There had made a lasting spring.
> Every thing that heard him play,
> Even the billows of the sea,
> > Hang their heads, and then lay by.
> In sweet music is such art,
> Killing care and grief of heart
> > Fall asleep, or hearing die.

HENRY VIII

In scene 3 the growing custom of imitating the
French in things musical, as well as in other
fashions, is sneeringly referred to by Sir Thomas
Lovell :

A French song and a fiddle has no fellow.

Great interest attaches to the passage in Act
IV, sc. 2, where Katharine makes request :

> Good Griffith,
> Cause the musicians play me that sad note
> I named my knell, whilst I sit meditating
> On that celestial harmony I go to.

> (*Sad and solemn music*)

Many have been the guesses and suggestions as to what the 'knell' so beloved by the queen was, some arguing for one piece, and some for another. It is a point impossible to settle.

JULIUS CÆSAR

There are but three or four references to Music in this Tragedy. The only important one is in Act I, sc. 2, where Cæsar indicates that men lacking in love for music are dangerous, and to be avoided:

Cæsar : Yet if my name were liable to fear,
I do not know the man I should avoid
So soon as that spare Cassius. He reads much;
He is a great observer, and he looks
Quite through the deeds of men : he loves no
    plays,
As thou dost, Anthony ; *he hears no music :*

In Act IV, sc. 3 the soothing effect of music is noted. Brutus asks his servant boy Lucius to sing to him, to his own accompaniment on the lute.

Brutus : Canst thou hold up thy heavy eyes
    awhile,
And touch thy instrument a strain or two.
Luc. : Ay, my lord, an't please you.
Bru. : It does, my boy :

I trouble thee too much, but thou art willing.
 Luc. : It is my duty, sir.
 Bru. : I should not urge thy duty past thy
  might ;
I know young bloods look for a time of rest.
 Luc. : I have slept, my lord, already.
 Bru. : It was well done ; and thou shalt sleep
  again ;
I will not hold thee long : if I do live,
I will be good to thee. (*Music and a song*)
This is a sleepy tune. O murderous slumber,
Lay'st thou thy leaden mace upon my boy,
That plays thee music. Gentle knave, good
  night ;
I will not do thee so much wrong to wake thee.

Timon of Athens

 A Mask of Ladies as Amazons, with lutes in
their hands, dancing and playing, and under the
direction of Cupid, visit the banquetting-hall
of Timon, and Timon, bidding them welcome,
says ' Music, make their welcome '.

Coriolanus

 In Act V, sc. 4, when the second Messenger
enters, he says :
    Why, hark you !

 (*Trumpets : hautboys ; drums beat ; all together*)

The trumpets, sackbuts, psalteries and fifes,
Tabors and cymbals and the shouting Romans,
Make the sun dance.   Hark you! (*A shout within*)

The only music attached to this Play is instrumental, and that is of the scantiest.

KING LEAR

To the musician or music-lover there is really
nothing of importance in this, Shakespeare's
greatest achievement perhaps, in Tragedy.   It
is interesting to note that the only songs introduced into the Play are rendered by the Fool
who ' is one of Shakespeare's triumphs ', and
without whom the harmony of the Play would be
sadly spoiled.

In Act I, sc. 4 he sings :

Fools had ne'er less wit in a year;
For wise men are grown foppish,
And know not how their wits to wear,
Their manners are so apish.

Lear : When were you wont to be so full of
songs, sirrah ?
Fool : I have used it, nuncle, ever since thou
madest thy daughters thy mother : for when thou
gavest them the rod and puttest down thine
own breeches.

(*Singing*) Then they for sudden joy did weep,
    And I for sorrow sung,
  That such a king should play bo-peep,
    And go the fools among.

Again, in Act III, sc. 2 :
  The cod-piece that will house
    Before the head has any,
  The head and he shall louse
    So beggars marry many.

  The man that makes his toe
    What he his heart should make
  Shall of a corn cry woe,
    And turn his sleep to wake.

And finally a little farther on in the same scene he sings :

  He that has and a little tiny wit—
  With hey, ho, the wind and the rain,—
  Must make content with his fortunes fit,
  For the rain it raineth every day.

TITUS ANDRONICUS
TROILUS AND CRES-
   SIDA
RICHARD III
CYMBELINE
PERICLES
HAMLET
MACBETH
ROMEO AND JULIET

CHAPTER VIII

Kinder all earth hath grown since genial
Shakespeare sung.

Lord Lytton.

Shakespeare! loveliest of souls,
Peerless in radiance, in joy.

Matthew Arnold

Titus Andronicus

THIS tragedy is practically devoid of musical interest.

Troilus and Cressida

Professor Dowden has called this ' the comedy of disillusion ', and he believed that ' this strange and difficult play was a last attempt to continue comedy made when Shakespeare had ceased to be able to smile genially, and when he must be either ironical, or else take a deep, passionate and tragical view of life '. There is a striking resemblance in the spirit and structure of this play to the tragedy of Timon of Athens, but there is a little more in its pages to interest the music-lover than in the former.

In the conversation between Pandarus and Helen, the former says:

Come, come, I'll hear no more of this; I'll sing you a song now.

> *Helen:* Let thy song be love: this love will undo us all.
>> O Cupid, Cupid, Cupid!
>
> *Pan:* Love! ay, that it shall, i' faith.
>
> *Paris:* Ay, good now, love, love, nothing but love.
>
> *Pan.:* In good truth, it begins so. (*Sings*)

> Love, love, nothing but love, still more!
>> For, O, love's bow
>> Shoots buck and doe:
>> The shaft confounds,
>> Not that it wounds,
> But tickles still the sore.

> These lovers cry Oh! oh! they die:
>> Yet that which seems the wound to kill,
> Doth turn oh! oh! to ha! ha! ha!
>> So dying love lives still:
> Oh! oh! a while, but ha! ha! ha!
> Oh! oh! groans out for ha! ha! ha!
> Heigh-ho!

> *Helen:* In love, i' faith, to the very tip of the nose.

(Act III, sc. 1)

Here, as in other plays, we have an interesting reference to ' broken music '.

Pan. : (Music within) What music is this ?

Serv. : I do but partly know, sir : it is music in parts.

Pan. : Know you the musicians ?

Serv. : Wholly, sir.

Pan. : Who play they to ?

Serv. : To the hearers, sir.

Pan. : At whose pleasure, friend ?

Serv. : At mine, sir, and theirs that love music

Enter Paris and Helen

Pan. : You speak your fair pleasure, sweet queen,

Fair Prince, here is good broken music.

Paris : You have broke it, cousin : and, by my life, you shall make it whole again ; you shall piece it out with a piece of your performance. Nell, he is full of harmony. . . .

Helen : We'll hear you sing, certainly.

(Act III, sc. 1)

RICHARD III

Music in this Play seems to be limited entirely to Alarums, Flourishes, and other instrumental effects. See Act III, sc. 1 ; Act IV. sc. 4.

The rare Stage direction of Sennet is used in this Play. (Act III, sc. 1)

CYMBELINE

This Play is of interest to all music-lovers, since it portrays for us in Imogen one of the most tender of female creations—so tender of rebukes that words are strokes, and strokes death to her—and is in itself a mine of poetry and musical speech.

In Act II, sc. 3 we have that charming song, which is notable to most people, because of its magnificent setting by Schubert. The original setting has been lost. Attached to the song there is a good deal of comment.

Cloten : I would this music would come . . .

Enter Musicians

Come on ; tune : if you can penetrate her with your fingering, so ; we'll try with tongue too : if none will do, let her remain ; but I'll never give o'er. First, a very excellent good-conceited thing ; after, a wonderful sweet air, with admirable rich words to it : and then let her consider.

Song

Hark, hark ! the lark at heaven's gate sings.
And Phœbus 'gins arise,

His steeds to water at those springs
On chaliced flowers that lies.
And winking Mary—buds begin
To ope their golden eyes ;
With every thing that pretty is,
My lady sweet, arise :
Arise ! Arise !

So get you gone. If this penetrate, I will consider your music the better : if it do not, it is a vice in her ears, which horse-hairs and calves'-guts, nor the voice of unpaved eunuch to boot, can never amend.

(*Exeunt Musicians*)

Dr Naylor points out that the mention of 'horse-hairs and calves'-guts' in this passage 'makes it clear that the instruments in this "morning music" were Viols'.

In Act IV, sc. 2 we have a song, or duet rather, sung by Guiderius and Arviragus, Cymbeline's two sons, in memory of Imogen. There is nothing earlier than an eighteenth-century setting to this most plaintive and moving dirge.

Song

Guid. : Fear no more the heat o' the sun,
Nor the furious winter's rages ;
Thou thy worldly task hast done,
Home art gone and ta'en thy wages

Golden lads and girls all must,
    As chimney-sweepers, come to dust.

Fear no more the frown o' the great ;
    Thou art past the tyrant's stroke ;
Care no more to clothe and eat ;
    To thee the reed is as the oak :
The sceptre, learning, physic, must
    All follow this and come to dust.

Guid. : Fear no more the lightning-flash,
Arvir. :   Nor the all-dreaded thunder-stone ;
Guid. : Fear not slander, censure rash ;
Arvir. :   Thou hast finish'd joy and moan :
Both : All lovers young, all lovers must
        Consign to thee and come to dust.
Guid. :   No exorciser harm thee !
Arvir. :   Nor nò witchcraft charm thee !
Guid. : Ghost unlaid forbear thee !
Arvir. :   Nothing ill come near thee !
Both : Quiet consummation have ;
    And renowned be thy grave.

PERICLES

This tragedy is fairly rich in musical allusions, some of them of very wide interest. It is here that we have one of the principal passages in Shakespeare on 'the music of the spheres'. Shakespeare apparently adopted the ancient

Pythagorean theory, namely, 'that the whole
world was constructed according to musical
ratio, and that the seven planets . . . have a
rhythmical motion and distances adapted to
musical intervals, and emit sounds, every one
different in proportion to its height, which
sounds are so concordant as to produce a most
sweet melody, though inaudible to us by reason
of the sounds, which the narrow passages of our
ears are not capable of admitting '.

The passage referred to above is in Act V, sc.
1, when Pericles discovers his long-lost daughter
Marina.

Per. :   I embrace you.
Give me my robes.   I am wild in my beholding.
O heavens bless my girl! But, hark, what
    music ?
Tell Helicanus, my Marina, tell him
O'er, point by point, for yet he seems to doubt,
How sure you are my daughter.   But, what
    music ?
    Hel. : My, lord, I hear none.
    Per. : None !
The music of the spheres !   List, my Marina.
    Lys. : It is not good to cross him ; give him
    way.
    Per. : Rarest sounds !   Do ye not hear ?

Lys. : My lord, I hear.

(Music)

Per. : Most heavenly music !
It nips me unto listening, and thick slumber
Hangs upon my eyes : let me rest.

(Sleeps)

The fabled magic power of music is illustrated
in the passage in Act III, sc. 2, where Cerimon,
a Lord of Ephesus, brings to life again the dead
Queen Thaisa who had been cast up by the sea.

The servants enter Cerimon's house bearing
a chest, which when opened proved to be a
coffin containing an embalmed corpse.

Cer. :   Make a fire within :
Fetch hither all my boxes in my closet.

(Exit a servant)

Death may usurp on nature many hours,
And yet the fire of life kindle again
The o'erpress'd spirits.   I heard of an Egyptian
That had nine hours lien dead,
Who was by good appliances recovered.

(Re-enter a servant, with boxes, napkins, and fire)

Well said, well said ; the fire and clothes.
The rough and woful music that we have,
Cause it to sound, beseech you.

The viol once more : how thou stirr'st, thou
    block !
The music there !
This queen will live. . .
       She hath not been entranced
Above five hours : see how she 'gins to blow
Into life's flower again !
  First Gent. :   The heavens,
Through you, increase our wonder, and set up
Your fame for ever.
  Cer. :   She is alive.

Here as in *Much Ado About Nothing*, and
elsewhere, we have a reference to music as a
decided accomplishment. Marina boasts to the
servant Boult :

Proclaim that I can sing, weave, sew, and dance,
With other virtues, which I'll keep from boast.

An ethical simile is introduced in Act I, sc. 1,
where unbridled passion is likened to bad and
tuneless music on the viol.

You are a fair viol and your sense the strings,
Who, finger'd to make man his lawful music,
Would draw heaven down and all the gods, to
    hearken,
But being play'd upon before your time,
Hell only danceth at so harsh a chime.

HAMLET

There is no lack of musical allusion in this wonderful tragedy, this 'marvel of subtle and penetrative thought, of tenderness, of humour ', which has been to the critics too often simply 'a wrangle over psychological problems '. The songs are allocated to Ophelia and the Clown.

The musicians, or singers rather, in the theatre of Shakespeare's day were men and boys, as no females were employed on the stage before the civil war. There is a highly interesting reference to the children of the stage and to their singing in Act II, sc. 2, where one of the Courtiers, Rosencrantz, gives an account of their work, and tells of their popularity, to Hamlet.

The Players are on the way to offer service to Hamlet. Hamlet inquires, 'What players are they ? '

Ros. : Even those you were wont to take such delight in, the tragedians of the city.

Ham. : How chances it they travel ? . . . . Do they hold the same estimation they did when I was in the city ? Are they so followed ?

Ros. : No, indeed, are they not.

Ham. : How comes it ? Do they grow rusty ?

Ros. : Nay, their endeavour keeps in the

wonted pace : but there is, sir, an eyrie of children,
little eyases, that cry out on the top of question
and are most tyrannically clapped for 't : these
are now the fashion, and so berattle the common
stages—so they call them—that many wearing
rapiers are afraid of goose-quills, and dare scarce
come thither.

Ham : What, are they children ? Who main-
tains them ? How are they escoted ? Will
they pursue the quality no longer than they can
sing ? Will they not say afterwards, if they
should grow themselves to common players—
as it is most like, if their means are no better
—their writers do them wrong, to make them
exclaim against their own succession ?

Ros. : Faith, there has been much to do on
both sides.

Elson interprets this passage to mean that
Shakespeare did not approve of children as actors.

In Act IV, sc. 5 we have these pathetically
trifling ditties which were sung by Ophelia
when her mind was off its balance through grief
and shame.

Queen : Let her come in.

Oph. : Where is the beauteous majesty of
Denmark ?

Queen : How now, Ophelia !

Oph. : (*sings*) How should I your true love know
From another one ?
By his cockle hat and staff
And his sandal shoon.[1]

Queen: Alas, sweet lady, what imports this song ?
Oph. : Say you ? nay, pray you, mark.

(*sings*) He is dead and gone, lady,
He is dead and gone ;
At his head a grass-green turf,
At his heels a stone.

Oh, oh !

Queen : Nay, but, Ophelia—
Oph. : Pray you, mark.

(*sings*) White his shroud as the mountain snow,

Enter King

Queen : Alas, look here, my lord.
Oph. : (*sings*) Larded with sweet flowers ;
Which bewept to the grave did go
With true-love showers.

King : How do you, pretty lady ?
Oph. : Well, God 'ild you ! They say the
owl was a baker's daughter. Lord, we know
what we are, but not what we may be. God be
at your table.

King : Conceit upon her father.

[1] The traditional music for this may be found on page 175.

Oph. : Pray you, let's have no words of this ; but when they ask you what it means, say you this :

(*sings*) To-morrow is Saint Valentine's day
    All in the morning betime,
And I a maid at your window,
    To be your Valentine.

Then up he rose, and donn'd his clothes,
    And dupp'd the chamber door ;
Let in the maid, that out a maid
    Never departed more.

King : Pretty Ophelia.

Ophelia sings, and then retires. A little later in the same scene she re-enters, and again takes up these irresponsible strains :

They bore him barefaced on the bier :
Hey non nonny, nonny, hey nonny :
And in his grave rained many a tear,—
    Fare you well, my dove !

You must sing down a-down,
  An you call him a-down-a.

O, how the wheel becomes it ! It is the false steward, that stole his master's daughter.

    And will a' not come again ?
    And will a' not come again ?

No, no, he is dead,
Go to thy death-bed,
He will never come again.

His beard was as white as snow,
All flaxen was his poll:
He is gone, he is gone,
And we cast away moan:
God ha' mercy on his soul!

And of all Christian souls, I pray God.   **God**
be wi' you.

While making a grave for Ophelia, one of **the**
clowns sings and digs:

In youth, when I did love, did love,
Methought it was very sweet,
To contract, O, the time, for—a my behove,
O, methought, there—a was nothing—a
meet.

But age, with his stealing steps,
Hath claw'd me in his clutch,
And hath shipped me intil the land,
As if I had never been such.

(throws up a skull)

A pick-axe, and a spade, a spade,
For and **a** shrouding sheet:

O, a pit of clay for to be made
For such a guest is meet.

(throws up another skull)

These lines callously hummed by the grave-digger were probably based on a ballad of the day which the ignorant clown had caught the sound of, if not the true sense.

MACBETH

In this ' tragedy of the twilight and the setting-in of thick darkness upon a human soul ', there is but little of a musical nature, as such, but incidental music has many times been set to the play.

In Act IV, sc. 1 a song is mentioned, namely ' Black Spirits, etc.', but so far as we know, no trace of the words as sung is now left.

ROMEO AND JULIET

The musical interest in this play is considerable. The only approach to singing is the lilt sung by Mercutio—Act II, sc. 4 :

An old hare hoar,
And an old hare hoar,
Is very good meat in Lent ;
But a hare that is hoar,
Is too much for a score,
When it hoars ere it be spent.

Romeo, will you come to your father's?
we'll to dinner thither.

Rom.: I will follow you.

Mer.: Farewell, ancient lady; farewell,

(*singing*) lady, lady, lady!

The passage in Act III, sc. 5 which speaks of
the parting of the lovers in Capulet's orchard, is
crowded with musical metaphor.

Rom.: It is not day.

Jul.: It is, it is; hie hence, be gone, away!
It is the lark that sings so out of tune.
Straining harsh discords and unpleasing sharps.
Some say the lark makes sweet division;
This doth not so, for she divideth us:
Some say the lark and loathed toad change eyes;
O, now I would they had changed voices too!
Since arm from arm that voice doth us affray,
Hunting thee hence with hunts-up to the day.
O, now be gone; more light and light it grows.

Rom.: More light and light: more dark and
dark our woes!

There is a musical allusion of no little interest
in a somewhat obscure passage in Act II, sc. 4
describing Tybalt, nephew to Lady Capulet.

Benvolio: Why, what is Tybalt?

Mercutio: More than prince of cats, I can tell

you. O, he's the courageous captain of compliments. He fights as you sing prick-song, keeps times, distance and proportion ; rests me his minim rest, one, two, and the third in your bosom : the very butcher of a silk button, a duellist, a duellist ; a gentleman of the very first house, of the first and second cause.

There is much musical quibbling, interspersed with a great deal of delicious sarcasm directed against both singers and instrumentalists, in Act IV, sc. 5.

> *First Mus. :* Faith, we may put up our pipes, and be gone.
> *Nurse :* Honest good fellows, ah, put up, put up ;
> For, well you know, this is a pitiful case.
> *First Mus. :* Ay, by my troth, the case may be amended.
>
> *Enter Peter*
>
> *Pet. :* Musicians, O, musicians, ' Heart's ease, Heart's ease ' ;
> O, an you will have me live, play ' Heart's ease ' ;[1]
> *First Mus. :* Why ' Heart's ease ' ?
> *Pet. :* O, musicians, because my heart itself plays ' My heart is full of woe,'
> O, play me some merry dump, to comfort me.

[1] The tune is given on page 180.

First Mus. : Not a dump we ; 'tis no time to play now.

Pet. : You will not then ?

First Mus. : No.

Pet. : I will then give it you soundly.

First Mus. : What will you give us ?

Pet. : No money, on my faith, but the gleek ; I will give you the minstrel.

First Mus. : Then will I give you the serving-creature.

Pet. : Then will I lay the serving-creature's dagger on your pate.   I will carry no crotchets : I'll *re* you, I'll *fa* you ; do you note me ?

First Mus. : An you *re* us and *fa* us, you note us.

Sec. Mus. : Pray you, put up your dagger, and put out your wit.

Pet. : Then have at you with my wit ! I will dry-beat you with an iron wit, and put up my iron dagger.   Answer me like men :

 ' When griping grief the heart doth wound
 And doleful dumps the mind oppress,
 The music with her silver sound '—
Why ' silver sound ' ?   why ' music with her silver sound ' ?   What say you, Simon Cat-ling ?

First Mus. : Marry, sir, because silver hath a sweet sound.

Pet. : Pretty !   What say you, Hugh Rebeck ? [1]

Sec. Mus. : I say, ' silver sound ' ;   because musicians sound for silver.

Pet. : Pretty too !   What say you, James Soundpost ?

Third Mus. : Faith, I know not what to say.

Pet. : O, I cry you mercy ;   you are the singer :   I will say for you.   It is ' music with her silver sound ' ;   because musicians have no gold for sounding :

> ' Then music with her silver sound
> With speedy help doth lend redress.'
>
> (Exit)

First Mus. : What a pestilent knave is this same !

Sec. Mus. : Hang him, Jack !   Come, we'll in here ;   tarry for the mourners, and stay dinner.

(Exeunt)

---

[1] It is noteworthy that Peter nicknames the three musicians, Catling, Rebeck and Soundpost respectively—all three being musical terms.

SHAKESPEARE AND
THE SONG-BIRDS

L

CHAPTER IX

Do you ne'er think what wondrous beings these?
Do you ne'er think who made them and who taught
The dialect they speak where melodies
  Alone are the interpreters of thought?   ·
Whose household words are songs in many keys,
  Sweeter than instrument of man e'er caught.
                              Longfellow.

SHAKESPEARE AND THE SONG-BIRDS

REFERENCE has already been made to the astounding receptivity of the mind of Shakespeare.   And as he was apparently observant to a singular degree, it is no matter for surprise that he should have paid special attention to the song-birds which in very large numbers no doubt haunted the leafy shades of Warwickshire in the poet's day.   Like Milton, Keats, Shelley, and many other poets, he was indebted to these charming denizens of the woods and hedgerows for inspiration and uplift, and like them he acclaims their service to his genius and art with a full meed of praise.⁖ The lark comes in for much attention.   Many of the metaphors and illustrations connected with the famed songster come to mind, e.g. :

Stir with the lark to-morrow, gentle Norfolk.
Rich. III, V, 3

I do hear the morning lark.
Mids. Night's Dream, IV, 1

The busy day, wak'd by the lark.
Troil. and Cres., IV, 2

Lo, here the gentle lark, weary of rest,
From his moist cabinet mounts on high,
And wakes the morning, from whose silver breast
The sun ariseth in his majesty.
Ven. & Adon., line 853

It was the lark, the herald of the morn, no nightingale.
Rom. & Jul., III, 5

All these references indicate the lark as the ' bird of dawn '.

The beautiful idea of the lark as climbing and climbing until it reaches the very gates of heaven, where it pours forth its song, is given expression to by the Poet on two occasions at least. In the famous song from *Cymbeline*, ' Hark, hark, the lark at heaven's gate sings ', and again in one of the sonnets.

Like to the lark, at break of day arising
From sullen earth, sings hymns at heaven's
gate.

The joy and buoyancy of the little brown
songster is referred to in *Love's Labour Lost:*

When shepherds pipe on oaten straws,
And merry larks are ploughmen's clocks.

In *Romeo and Juliet* the lark is spoken of as
giving out harsh notes, and singing out of tune,
but the remarks of Juliet are ill-natured and
untrue. She is angry with the poor bird because
his song proclaims the hour when she must part
from her lover. In her spite she said she would
prefer to hear the croak of the toad to the song
of the lark, since that would have been no sign
of the approach of day, and so no signal for her
lover to be off.
(Act III, sc. 5)

There are other references to the lark in
The Winter's Tale, IV, 2 :

The lark that tirra-lirra chants.

Rich. II, III, 3 :

For night-owls shriek, where mounting larks
should sing.

Lear, IV, 6 :

The shrill-gorg'd lark.

A curious old method of snaring the lark is brought before us in the lines in *Henry VIII*, Act III, sc. 2 :

> Let his grace go forward,
> And dare us with his cap, like larks.

A small piece of red cloth, together with a piece of looking-glass, were moved about within sight of the bird, and at a little distance from the fowler, and when the birds, through curiosity, came within range, they were cleverly netted. The cap mentioned was, of course, the scarlet hat of the Cardinal.

THE THRUSH

This brilliant songster is only referred to on two or three occasions, In *The Merchant of Venice* Portia speaks of the French Lord Le Bon, and no doubt, in allusion to his national ' propensity for a dance on every possible occasion ', she says (Act I, sc. 2) :

> If a throstle sing, he falls straight a-capering.

And again in *A Midsummer Night's Dream*, Act III, sc. 1 Bottom sings of

> The throstle, with his note so true.

Whether Bottom be right or not, it is certainly held by some that the thrush, with his clear, rich, loud notes, takes a very high place among our feathered singers.

THE CUCKOO

The cuckoo, that bird of historic interest and reputedly varied gifts as a singer, is repeatedly mentioned in Shakespeare's plays. The references are, we fear, not at all complimentary. The evil reputation of the cuckoo for ingratitude and selfishness is referred to in *King Lear* (Act I, sc. 4), when the Fool reminds Lear that it is in the hedge-sparrow's nest that the cuckoo frequently lays its eggs, and is then so ungrateful for the benefit that her young eat off the head of the bird which has so helped her; and again in *Henry IV* (Act V, Part 1, sc. 1) Worcester says :

And being fed by us, you us'd us so
As that ungentle gull, the cuckoo's bird,
Useth the sparrow ; did oppress our nest,
Grew by our feeding to so great a bulk,
That even our love durst not come near your
    sight,
For fear of swallowing.

The musical notes of the cuckoo, or rather the notes of cuckoo which are so wanting in music, give rise to many a joke and gibe.

He knows me as the blind man knows the cuckoo,
By the bad voice.

Merch. of Ven., Act V, sc. 1

The plain song cuckoo gray,
Whose note full many a man doth mark,
And dares not answer, nay—

for, indeed, who would set his wish to so foolish
a bird ? who would give a bird the lie, though he
cry ' cuckoo ' never so ?

Mids. Night's Dream, Act III, sc. 1

A friend of the noted Gilbert White of Selborne found that the notes of different cuckoos varied greatly in quality and compass. In and round Selborne Wood the notes were mostly in D. On one occasion he heard two birds sing together, the one in D and the other in E flat, which, it is easy to understand, made anything but an agreeable duet. Gungl, in his ' Cuckoo Galop ', gives the notes of the cuckoo as B natural and G sharp. Dr Arne, when setting his music to the cuckoo's song in *Love's Labour's Lost*, put them as C natural and G.

The Robin

The robin, or ruddock as it is still called in some parts of England, has been immortalized in these lovely and pathetic lines in *Cymbeline*.

With fairest flowers
Whilst summer lasts, and I live here Fidels,
I'll sweeten thy sad grave : thou shalt not lack
The Flower that's like thy face, pale primrose, nor
The azur'd harebell, like thy veins ; no, nor
The leaf of eglantine, whom not to slander,
Out-sweeten'd not thy breath ; the ruddock
    would,
With charitable bill,—O, bill, sore-shaming
Those rich-left heirs that let their fathers lie
Without a monument ! bring thee all this ;
Yea, and furr'd moss besides, when flowers are
    none,
To winter-ground thy corse.
                    Cymbeline, Act IV, sc. 2

Our popular little songster is referred to under
his own proper name in *Two Gentlemen of Verona*,
Act II, sc. 1 :

To relish a love-song like a robin-redbreast.

THE WREN

The courageous little wren is repeatedly introduced to the reader of Shakespeare, and her
appearance is more than once associated with
bravery and consummate daring. In *Macbeth*,
Act IV, sc. 1 we are told that

The poor wren, the most diminutive of birds,
    will fight,
Her young ones in her nest, against the owl.

And in *Rich. III*, Act I, sc. 3 :

A wren may prey where eagles dare not perch.

Portia evidently had no high opinion of the wren's song (*Merch. of Ven.*, Act V, sc. 1), but, though there may not be much variety in the tones, they are wonderfully strong, and compel attention.

THE NIGHTINGALE

The nightingale seems to have been the first favourite in all the ' feathered singing throng ' among the poets, some of whom have sung of her glorious song in undying lines. There are many most interesting allusions to this far-famed bird in the work of Shakespeare. If Shakespeare was the author of Section XIX of *The Passionate Pilgrim*, then he must have been familiar with the old fable which stated that the mournful notes of this mysterious bird were caused by the bird's pressing against a sharp thorn while she sang. The idea is poetic enough, but we live in unpoetic days, and we fear it is a fact that such a belief had its rise from the habit of the bird frequenting thorny copses, and building her nest amongst brambles on the ground.

When we remember that the name Philomel is often applied to the nightingale, we notice that the poetic idea mentioned above comes into play in *The Rape of Lucrece.*

And whiles against a thorn thou bear'st thy part,
To keep thy sharp woes waking.

Portia no doubt makes a point when she says that if the nightingale were to sing during the day she would be considered no better a musician than the wren. While the nightingale sings oftenest at nighttime, it is nevertheless a well-established fact that she sings as sweetly and powerfully oftentimes by day. It is no doubt one of her principal charms that she alone among the songsters keeps her best songs for eventide, when her human audience can hear without interruption from other birds. We speak under correction, but we believe that the male bird only is the songster. The origin of the change of sex has been attributed to an old fable which tells of the transformation of Philomela, daughter of Pandion, one of the Kings of Athens, into a nightingale, when Progne, her sister, was transformed into a swallow. (See Ovid's *Metamorphoses*, Book VI, Fable 6)

Mention is made of the nightingale in *Two Gentlemen of Verona*, Act III, sc. 1 :

> Except I be by Sylvia in the night,
> There is no music in the nightingale.

And in Act V, sc. 4:

> Here can I sit alone, unseen of any,
> And to the nightingale's complaining notes
> Tune my distresses and record my woes.

Mids. Night's Dream, Act I, sc. 2:
I will roar you an 'twere any nightingale.

Taming of the Shrew, Induction, sc. 2:
Apollom plays, and twenty caged nightingales
  do sing.

Lear, Act III, sc. 6:
The foul fiend haunts poor Tom in the voice
  of a nightingale.

Taming of the Shrew, Act II, sc. 1:
Say, that she rail; why, then I'll tell her plain,
She sings as sweetly as a nightingale.

There are other 'light-wing'd Dryads of the trees' which come in for more or less attention from our all-observing Bard, such as the Blackbird or Ouzel-cock, the Finch, the Sparrow or Philip; but we have dealt more particularly with those which claim Shakespeare's greatest attention.

MUSICAL   INSTRU-
MENTS IN PLAYS
AND POEMS

CHAPTER X

All lutes, all harps, all viols, all flutes, all lyres,
Fall dumb before him ere one string suspires.
   All stars are angels ; but the sun is God.
                                    Swinburne.

MUSICAL INSTRUMENTS IN PLAYS AND POEMS

The Viol

THE viol was far and away the most popular
stringed instrument played with a bow
in Shakespeare's day, and there are many allusions
to it in his works. It was considered to be part
of a good education to be able to play on the
viol. When Maria called Sir Andrew Aguecheek
' a fool ', Sir Toby Belch defended him thus—
' Fye, that you'll say so ! he plays o' the viol-
de-gamboys, and speaks three or four languages
word for word without book, and hath all the
good gifts of nature '. (*Twelfth Night*, Act I,
sc. 3.) Similes to playing on the viol are used
in *Richard II*, Act I, sc. 3, when the Duke of
Norfolk is sentenced to banishment :

' A heavy sentence, my most sovereign liege,
And one unlooked for from your highness' mouth :
A dearer merit, not so deep a maim
As to be cast forth in the common air,
Have I deserved at your highness' hand.
The language I have learned these forty years,
My native English, now I must forego :
And now my tongue's use is to me no more,
Than an unstringed viol or a harp ;
Or, like a cunning instrument cased up,
Or, being open, put into his hands,
That knows no touch to tune the harmony.

And in *Pericles* (Act I, sc. I) the Prince of
Tyre addresses the daughter of Antiochus as
follows :

You are a fair viol and your sense the strings,
Who, finger'd to make man his lawful music,
Would draw heaven down and all the gods, to
     hearken,
But being play'd upon before your time,
Hell only danceth at so harsh a chime.

The viol was of three different sizes, the
treble, the tenor, and the bass, corresponding
as nearly as may be to our modern violin, viola,
and violoncello. The bass viol was also known
as the Viol da Gamba, as it was held between

the knees. The viol differed from the violin in having six strings instead of four, and the viol family had frets on the finger-boards to mark out the notes, whereas the finger-board of the violin is quite smooth and gives no help to the player in that respect. The viols were used mainly for part-music, and the Fantasia was the kind of music mostly written by the composers of the sixteenth century for that purpose.

THE LUTE

The lute was the common musical stringed instrument of the home in Shakespeare's time, as the pianoforte is the principal domestic musical instrument of ours. It was popular not only in England, but throughout nearly the whole of Europe. It was made in various sizes, and was mainly used to accompany songs, usually sung by the player himself, but it was often used also in chamber music to support the viols. Seldom perhaps was it used as a solo instrument. It figures largely in the plays of Shakespeare in connexion with 'serenading' when love-songs were to be sung outside the fair lady's chamber.

The strings of the lute were arranged in pairs tuned in unison, with a single string called the *chanterelle*, on which the melody was performed. Lute-strings were often given as presents. Eliza-

M

bethan gallants were wont to make up a packet
of lute-strings, tied together with a piece of
ribbon, conceal a love-ditty perhaps among
them, and send it as a special gift to the lady of
his choice. It is said that Queen Elizabeth
herself was very fond of receiving such presents,
constituting as they did, a tribute to her beauty
as well as to her musical ability.

There are several interesting references in
Shakespeare to the lute. In *Much Ado About
Nothing* Claudio makes fun of Benedick because
of the state of melancholy into which he has
fallen, and Don Pedro ascribes it to his having
fallen in love.

Claud.: Nay, but his jesting spirit; which is
now crept into a lute-string, and now governed
by stops.

D. Pedro: Indeed, that tells a heavy tale for
him: Conclude, conclude he is in love. (Act
III, sc. 2)

Lord Talbot soothes the dying Earl of Salis-
bury with the lines:
Salisbury, cheer thy spirit with this comfort;
Thou shalt not die whiles—
He beckons with his hand and smiles on me,
As who should say, 'When I am dead and gone,
Remember to avenge me on the French'.
Plantagenet, I will; and like thee, Nero,

Play on the lute, beholding the towns burn :
Wretched shall France be only in my name.
Henry VI, Part I, Act I, sc. 4

Lutes were very difficult to keep in tune, and
much time was consumed in retuning at changes
of key. An eighteenth-century writer on musical
matters—Johann Mattheson—says that ' if a
lute-player have lived eighty years, he has probably spent about sixty years tuning his instrument '. It is to this difficulty, no doubt, that
Bianca refers in the lines :

Why, gentlemen, you do me double wrong,
To strive for that which resteth in my choice :
I am no breeching scholar in the schools ;
I'll not be tied to hours nor 'pointed times,
But learn my lessons as I please myself.
And, to cut off all strife, here sit we down :
Take you your instrument, play you the whiles ;
His lecture will be done ere you have tuned.
The Taming of the Shrew, Act III, sc. 1

A lute usually composed part of the stock-
in-trade of a barber in Shakespeare's day ; the
waiting customer could while away the time by
discoursing music on the instrument. The frets
on the lute were strings of catgut, and as the
barber was often a dentist as well, he used a
broken lute-string wherewith to draw teeth ;

and sometimes he would hang one of those festooned with the teeth he had extracted, in the window of his shop.

The lute-player did not read his music from staves like other musicians; he had a complete notation of his own called a *tablature*, which has now fortunately become quite obsolete.

THE RECORDER

The recorder was a reed instrument belonging to the flute family, with a mouthpiece very much like that of the flageolet. It was noted for its sweet tone, and many seventeenth-century poets used the term ' record ' in speaking of the song of a bird, especially the nightingale. The recorder was principally used in part-music. All readers of *Hamlet* will recall the interesting and telling psychological remarks of the Prince of Denmark as he addresses Guildenstern on the playing of the recorder. (Act III, sc. 2)

Hamlet: O, the recorders—
(*to Guildenstern*) Will you play upon this pipe?
Guild.: My lord, I cannot.
Ham.: I pray you.
Guild.: I cannot.
Ham.: I do beseech you.
Guild.: I know no touch of it, my lord.
Ham.: 'Tis as easy as lying: govern these

ventages with your fingers and thumb, give it breath with your mouth, and it will discourse most excellent music. Look you, these are the stops.

Guild. : But these cannot I command to any utterance of harmony; I have not the skill.

Ham. : Why, look you now, how unworthy a thing you make of me. You would play upon me; you would seem to know my stops; you would pluck out the heart of my mystery; you would sound me from my lowest note to the top of my compass : and there is much music, excellent voice in this little organ; yet cannot you make it speak. 'Sblood, do you think, I am easier to be played on than a pipe? Call me what instrument you will, though you can fret me, you cannot play upon me.

A clever and humorous allusion is made to playing on the recorder in *Midsummer Night's Dream*. Quince having sadly muddled his declamation of the Prologue, Theseus says:

'This fellow doth not stand upon points', and Lysander adds the remark:

'He hath rid his prologue like a rough colt; he knows not the stop. A good moral, my lord : it is not enough to speak, but to speak true.'

Hippolyta contributes the diverting item to the conversation:

'Indeed he hath played on his prologue, like a child on a recorder; a sound, but not in government'. (Act V, sc. 1)

THE BAGPIPE

The bagpipe is referred to occasionally in the plays of Shakespeare. It is an instrument of great antiquity, and is found over a wide extent of the world. Chaucer mentions it as helping to pass the time, and cheering the steps of the weary Canterbury pilgrims. The instrument consists of a wind-bag which is usually filled from the mouth of the player, though sometimes, as in the case of the Irish bagpipe, the wind is supplied to the wind-bag by means of a pair of bellows worked by the pressure of the elbow : a reservoir to contain the wind, a certain number of the plain tubes forming the drones, which are not under any further control of the player; and the *chaunter*, a pierced tube on which the melody is performed. Some one has said that in the bagpipes we have the modern organ in embryo.

There are two allusions of special interest in the plays to the bagpipes, both surrounded by a good deal of mystery and difficulty, when we seek to explain them. The first is in *Henry IV*, Part I, Act I, sc. 2.

Falstaff: 'Sblood, I am melancholy as a gib cat or a lugged bear.

Prince: Or an old lion, or a lover's lute.

Fal.: Yes, or the drone of a Lincolnshire bagpipe.

One commentator explains this reference to the bagpipe as a jesting allusion to the frogs croaking in the Lincolnshire marshes, but Malone, who is a wonderfully safe guide on many intricate points, prefers the more feasible explanation that the Lincolnshire bagpipe was a well-known form of accompaniment to the common dancing which was so prevalent in the Fen country at festive seasons.

The second puzzling allusion to the bagpipe is in *The Merchant of Venice* (Act IV, sc. 1, line 56) where Shylock refers to a ' woollen bagpipe '. Some think that the reading should be ' swollen ' (as it is in several of the older editions of the Plays); others think that the adjective refers, not to the instrument itself, but to the woollen covering which often protected it.

The Virginal

In the first half of the sixteenth century attempts were made to apply keys to stringed instruments. The strings at first were of gut, but these were soon replaced with wire; the instrument was called the clavichord. The virginal was a modification of or adaptation from the clavichord, and was the most popular of all the keyboard musical instruments in Shakespeare's day, though it is nowhere directly mentioned in his works. It is supposed by some that the name of virginal was given to it in honour of Queen Elizabeth, the virgin queen, with whom it was a favourite. The tone of the virginal was rather faint, and the music it produced was for the boudoir, not for the theatre.

The only indirect reference to this very popular instrument which is to be found in Shakespeare is in *A Winter's Tale*. The jealous Leontes is watching Hermione, and when he sees her take the hand of Polixenes, he murmurs angrily—' Still virginalling upon his palm '. (Act I, sc. 2).

Dr. E. W. Naylor gives a technical description of the virginal in *The Musical Antiquary* of April, 1910 (page 129).

THE CORNET

The *cornet* of Elizabethan times was not the instrument known to us by that name. It was a kind of horn made of a hollowed tusk, or of wood covered with leather. It had a mouthpiece like the cup of a trumpet. It was bored with six holes on one side, covered by the fingers,

Viol da Gamba

Archlute

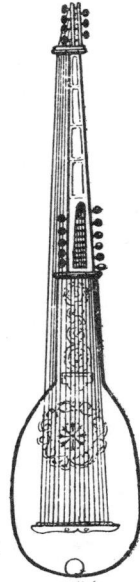

Virginals

[*Between pages* 168 *and* 169

Lute

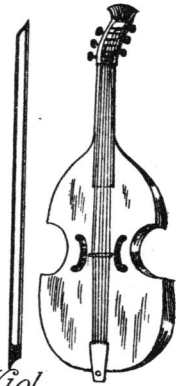

Viol

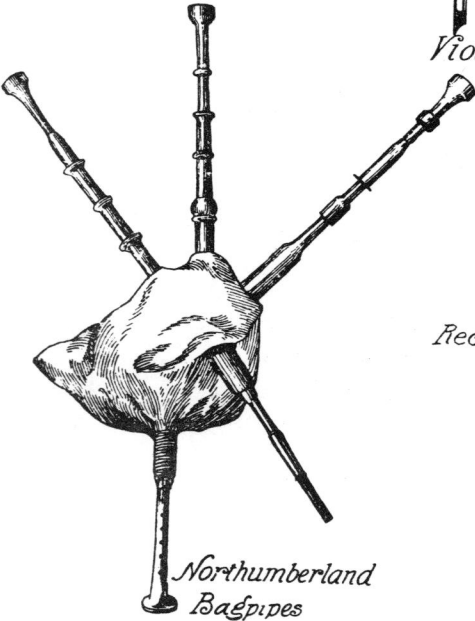

Recorder

Northumberland
Bagpipes

and with one hole on the reverse side, covered by the thumb. The tone was feeble and reed-like. Cornets were often used in private houses and small theatres, where the noisy din of brazen trumpets would have been unendurable.

The cornet is mentioned in the trial scene of Queen Katherine in *Henry VIII*, Act I, sc. 2 ; several times in *Coriolanus*, Act I, sc. 10. Act III, sc. 1 ; and in *The Merchant of Venice* cornets were employed for the casket scene, Act II.

TABOR AND FIFE

The tabor, a small hand-drum, was long popular in England, associated with the fife, both instruments usually being played by the same person. These have their counterpart in our day in the Drum and Fife band. The fife is repeatedly mentioned in Shakespeare, and his reference to the ' wry-necked fife ' in *The Merchant of Venice* (Act II, sc. 5) has given rise to considerable comment. Dr Naylor thinks the adjective ' wry-necked ' applies to the player and not to the instrument. The fife itself was straight, but it was held across the face of the player, whose head would be turned sideways, hence the description of the instrument as ' wry-necked '.

The Hautboy

The hautboy of Shakespeare's day was a conical wooden tube with six holes in front for the fingers and a thumb-hole at the back. It was popularly known by the name of 'wait' or 'shawm'. The tone was shrill and reedy. The treble hautboy was practically the same as the shepherd's pipe. Hautboys were almost always played in 'consorts or families'. The tenor hautboy has developed into our cor-anglais, while the bass has become our bassoon. There are many references in Shakespeare to the hautboy. In order to get a grand musical effect when Coriolanus and his Volscians leave Rome, the stage-direction provides that:

Trumpets, Hoboyes, Drums beate altogether (Coriolanus, Act V, sc. 4).

Other references to the hautboy may be found in *Macbeth*, Act I, sc. 6, *Henry VIII*, Act I, sc. 4, *Timon of Athens*, Act I, sc 2.

Other instruments mentioned in the plays and poetry of Shakespeare are the organ, the cittern, the serpent (now obsolete), and the trumpet. The directions in the Plays for 'flourishes', 'sennets', and the 'sounding of trumpets' are far too numerous to mention.

APPENDICES.

Appendix I

THE following musical examples represent some of the chief traditional tunes used or referred to by Shakespeare. The first, ' O, how should I your true love know ', is one of the many snatches of song which Shakespeare introduces to illustrate the madness of Ophelia. Ophelia's ditties were all well-known street songs, and Shakespeare does not hesitate to put the tunes of these lewd ditties on the lips of the lovely Ophelia in order to emphasize her dire affliction. The second— the Willow Song—which was a favourite with Desdemona's mother's maid, was also a folk song well known in Elizabethan days, and probably even then of long standing. There are many varied readings of it. ' O, Mistress mine ! ' was another well-known ditty of the time. It was utilized by Morley and others in their madrigals. The B natural in bar 2 of the voice part is truer to the custom of the times than the more ordinary B flat. This song is sung by the Clown on the invitation of Sir Andrew Aguecheek (*see* page 32). ' Heart's ease ' was another favourite in Shakespeare's day. It is referred to in *Romeo and Juliet* (*see* page 141). The lively tune of Greensleeves is alluded to in *The Merry Wives of Windsor*. The minor key was not then so closely associated with sadness as it is too frequently nowadays. Catch-singing was much in use in Elizabethan times, and was introduced not infrequently on the stage. Catches were popular songs much in favour at the merrymakings of rude but jolly people. Two of the oldest catches preserved are here appended.

Ophelia's Street Song.

In moderate time

O how should I your true love know, From an - oth - er

one? Oh by his san - dal, hat and staff, And his

san - dal shoon.   *(Symphony)*

Desdemona's Willow Song.

(Othello.)

Traditional Air
(Harmony by A. EAGLEFIELD HULL).

willow, willow, willow,　willow, My gar-land must be,　Sing
all　a green wil-low,　wil-low, willow, wil-low,　Ah
me,　The green, green wil-low my gar-land must be.

O Mistress Mine.

Clown's Song in " Twelfth Night."

Air, traditional
(Harmony by A. EAGLEFIELD HULL)

Gently swinging

O mis-tress mine,

Where are you roaming? O stay and hear, Your true love's com-ing,

O stay and hear, Your true love's coming, That can sing both high and low. Trip no fur-ther, pret - ty sweet - ing,

Journ - eys! end in lov-ers' meet-ing, Ev' - ry wise man's

son . . . doth know

The Old Tune: " Heart's-ease."

The Tune of "Greensleeves."

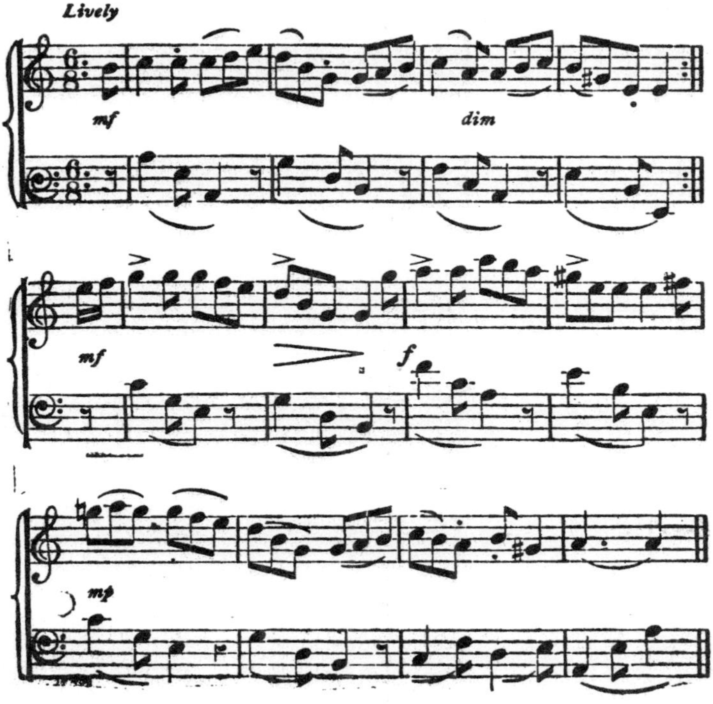

Catch: "Thou Knave."

(16th century.)

Hold thy peace and I pri-thee hold thy peace

Thou knave   hold thy peace,   thou knave

Thou knave

Catch: "Ding, dong bell."

(15th century.)

All   in - to   ser - - vice

Let us sing merri - ly   to - geth -

er;   Ding, ding, ding, dong bell.

Appendix II

MUSIC AND SHAKESPEARE

ANTONY AND CLEOPATRA

Come thou monarch of the vine.
Bishop, H. R. Trio, A.T.B.

AS YOU LIKE IT

Blow, blow, thou winter wind.
Arne, T. A.   Song for Tenor.
Arne, T. A., and Bishop, H. R.   Part-Song, S.A.T.B.
Bartholomew, A. M.   Part-Song, A.T.T.B.
Beck-Slinn, E.   'Shakespeare Songs.'
Bishop, H. R.   Part-Song, A.T.T.B.
Crow, E. J.   Trio, S.S.C.
Duncan, Edmondstoune, for Bass or Baritone.
Hoby, Charles.   Two-Part Song.
Hotham, Charles.   For Contralto or Baritone.
Kilburn, N.   Part-Song, S.A.T.B.
Macfarren, G. A.   Part-Song, S.A.T.B.
Parry, C. H. H.
Stevens, R. J. S.
Wood, C.   Part-Song, S.A.T.B.
Zimmerman, Agnes.   Song for Bass.

It was a lover and his lass.
>   Austin, Frederick. Song.
>   Barnby, J. Part-Song, S.A.T.B.
>   Beck-Slinn, E. Song.
>   Booth, Josiah.
>   Brewer, A. Herbert.
>   Bridge, J. C.
>   Bright, Dora.
>   Cardew, Herbert W.
>   Dannreuther, E.
>   German, E.
>   Linton, A. H.
>   Macfarren, G. A.
>   Morley, T. The earliest known setting.
>   (See *Three Shakespeare Songs.* A. E. Hull.)
>   Ogilvy, A. W.
>   Reay, S.
>   Reynolds, C. T.
>   Rodgers, John.
>   Selby, B. Luard.
>   Stevens, R. J. S.
>   Richardson, A. M.
>   Wood, Charles.

Under the Greenwood Tree.
>   Anstruther, P. N. Part-Song.
>   Arne, T. A. Song for Tenor.
>   Arne, T. A., and Bishop, R. H. Glee, A.T.T.B.
>   Bantock, Granville.
>   Hoby, Charles. Two-Part Song.
>   Hotham, Charles. Song for Contralto or Baritone.
>   Lehmann, Liza. Part-Song.
>   Linton, A. H. Two Equal Voices.
>   Macfarren, G. A. Part-Song.
>   Ogilvy, A. W. Part-Song.

Parry, C. H. H.   Song.
Richards, A.   Two-Part Song.
Richardson.
Shaw, James.   Part-Song.
Wareing, H. W.   Part-Song.
Wood, C.   Two-Part Song.
Wurm, Marie.   Part-Song.

Wedding is great Juno's crown.
Tours, Berthold.   Chorus.

What shall he have that killed the Deer ?
Bishop, H. R.   Glee and Chorus.
Lowe, C. Egerton.   Unison Song.
Smith, J. S.   Trio, S.S.B.
Gadsby, H.   Orchestral Scene, 'The Forest of Arden.'
German, E.   Masque Music.

Fear no more the heat o' the sun.
Cardew, Herbert W.   Song for Contralto or Bass.
Macfarren, G. A.   Part-Song.
Tours, B.   Melodrama Music for this, when spoken instead of sung (Strings).

Hark the Lark.
Bright, Dora.   Song for Soprano.
Clarke, J. Hamilton.   Part-Song.
Cooke, B.   Part-Song.
Glendinning, R. R.   Song for Mezzo-Soprano.
Kerr, Lord Mark.   Song for Mezzo-Soprano.
Kucken, F.   Part-Song.
Locknane, C.
Macfarren, G. A.
Schubert, F.   Song.
Thorne, E. H.   Part-Song.

HAMLET

Incidental Music.

German, E. Symphonic Poem.
Henschel, G. Suite.
Tours, B. Incidental Music for Violin and Piano.
O'Neill, Norman. Overture, Danish Dance, Dirge.

HENRY THE FOURTH (PART I)

She bids you upon the wanton rushes lay you down.

Rogers, L. J. Part-Song.

HENRY THE FOURTH (PART II)

O sleep, O gentle sleep.

Leslie, H. Part-Song.

HENRY THE EIGHTH

Fox, Arthur. Vision Music.
German, E. Incidental Music.
  Overture.
  Three Dances.
  Prelude to Act II.
  Prelude to Act III.
  Prelude to Act IV.
  Prelude to Act V.
  Coronation March and Hymn.

Orpheus with his lute.

Aspa, E. Song for Soprano.
Baines, Herbert. Song for Soprano.
Beck Slinn.
Brewer, A. H. Song for Soprano or Tenor.
German, E. Trio.

Greatorex. Song for Soprano.
Hatton, J. L. Two-Part Song.
Macfarren, G. A. Part-Song.
Mainzar. (In sweet music). Two-Part Song,
    unaccompanied.
Sullivan.

LOVE'S LABOUR'S LOST

If she be made of white and red.

Dannreuther, E. Duet, Mezzo-Soprano and
    Baritone.
Sidebotham, M. A. Trio, Treble Voices.

So sweet a kiss.

Sampson, G. Part-Song.

When daisies pied.

Arne, T. A. Song for Soprano.
Dannreuther, E. Duet, S.B.
Macfarren, G. A. Part-Song.
Muller, J. Part-Song.

When icicles hang by the wall.

Arne, T. A. Song for Tenor.
Baines, Herbert. Song for Mezzo-Soprano.
Brooks, W. W. Part-Song.
Dannreuther, E. Duet.
Duncan, E. Part-Song.
Gardiner, H. Balfour. Song.
Lehmann, Liza. Part-Song.
Macfarren, G. A. Part-Song.
Parry.
Simpson, F. J. Trio.

MACBETH

Incidental Music attributed to Matthew Locke.

When shall we three meet again?
　　Horsley, W.
　　King, N. P.

MEASURE FOR MEASURE

Take, oh, take those lips away.
　　Iles, E.　Madrigal.
　　Macfarren, G. A.　Part-Song.
　　Macirone, C. A.
　　Parry, C. H. H.
　　Prendagast, A. H. D.
　　Reay, S.　Part-Song.
　　Taylor, J. A.　Song for Soprano or Tenor.
　　Wilson, J.　The earliest known setting.

MERCHANT OF VENICE

How sweet the moonlight sleeps upon this bank.
　　Callcott, J. G.　Part-Song.
　　Evans, D. Emlyn.　Part-Song.
　　Faning, Eaton.　Eight-Part Song.
　　Leslie, H.　Part-Song.
　　Wood, C.　Part-Song.

Let me play the fool.
　　Leslie, H.　Part-Song.
　　Pinsuti, C.　Part-Song.

Tell me where is fancy bred?
　　Bartholomew, A. M.　Part-Song.
　　Beck-Slinn, E.

Callcott, J. G. Trio.
Knight, Richard.
Lehmann, Liza. Part-Song.
Lutgen, B. Duettomo with Chorus.
Macfarren, G. A. Part-Song
Pinsuti, C. Part-Song.

MERRY WIVES OF WINDSOR

O by rivers.
    Bishop, H. R. Part-Song.

MIDSUMMER NIGHT'S DREAM

Mendelssohn's *Incidental Music.*
    Overture.
    Intermezzo.
    Notturno.
    Scherzo.
    Wedding March.
    You spotted snakes.
    Thro' the house.

I know a bank.
    Horn, C. A. Two-Part Song.
    Lehmann, Liza. Part-Song.

O happy fair.
    Shield, W. Glee.

Over hill, over dale.
    Attwater, J. P. Two-Part Song.
    Burnett, E. Part-Song.
    Hatton, J. L.
    Lloyd, C. H. Two-Part Song.

Through the Forest.
Gattie, J. B. Unison Song.

Trip Away.
Horn, C. A. Solo and Chorus.

You spotted snakes.
Brian Havergal.
Davis, J. D. Soprano Solo.
Lutgen, B. Part-Song.
Macfarren, G. A. Part-Song.
Mendelssohn (see above).
St. Mundella, R. Two-Part Song.
Stevens, R. J. S. Glee.

Titania. Opera by G. Huë.
Oberon. Operas by Wranetzky (1790), by Kunzen (1790) and Weber (1825).

MUCH ADO ABOUT NOTHING

Sigh no more, ladies.
Austin, Frederick. Song in D and F
Arne.
Beck-Slinn, E.
Baines, Herbert.
Fox, A. Song for Medium Voice.
Lovatt, S. E. Part-Song.
Macfarren, G. A. Part-Song.
Stevens, R. J. S. Part-Song.
Sullivan, Sir A.
Richardson.
German, E. Incidental Music.

OTHELLO

And let me the canakin clink.
Baines, Herbert.
McEwen, J. B. Part-Song.

O, willow, willow.

> Traditional. See *Three Shakespeare Songs* (A. E. Hull).
> Humfrey, P.
> Mackenzie, A. C.
> Parry, C. H.

RICHARD THE THIRD

Overture.

> German, Edward.

ROMEO AND JULIET

Incidental Music.

> German, E. 1, Prelude ; 2, Pastorale ; 3, Pavane ; 4, Nocturne ; 5, Dramatic Interlude. Tours, B. Incidental Music. Strings and Piano MS.

TAMING OF THE SHREW

Incidental Music, Wight, A. N.

Should he upbraid.

> Bishop, H. R. Song for Soprano.

TIMON OF ATHENS

Purcell, Henry. Full Score-Purcell Society.

THE TEMPEST

Incidental Music.

> Sullivan, Arthur.
> > Three Dances.
> > Banquet Dance.

Dance of Nymphs and Reapers.
Overture.
Prelude.
Dunstan, R.   The Tempest.
Selected and arranged for the use of Schools.

Come unto these yellow sands.
Banister, J.   The earliest known setting.
Corder, F.
Dansie, Redgewell.
Sullivan, A.   Soprano Solo and Chorus.

Full fathom five.
Banister, J.
Grosvenor, Hon. Norman.
Ireland, John.
Johnson, R.
Mangelsdorff, A.   Madrigal
Purcell, H.
Richardson, A. M.
Sullivan, A.   Soprano Solo and Chorus.
Vicars, G. R.
Wood, C.   Part-Song.

Honour, riches, marriage-blessing.
Shield, W.   Two-Part Song.
Sullivan, A.   Duet.

The cloud-capt towers.
Stevens, R. J. S.

Where the bee sucks.
Arne, T. A.
Bantock.
Corder, F.

Humfrey, Pelham.
Johnson, Richard.
Schartau, H.   Two-Part Song.
Sullivan, A.   Soprano Solo.

Inspired by *The Tempest.*
Beethoven's F Minor Sonata, Opus 57.
Bonnet's *Elves* (Ariel) for Organ.

TWELFTH NIGHT

Overture.
Mackenzie, A. C.

Come away, Death.
Arne, T. A.   Part-Song.
Brahms, J.   Trio.
Corder, F.   Trio.
Davies, G. Walford.   Song for Tenor.
Drayton, H. U.   Song.
Harrison, Julius.   Trio.
Macfarren, G. A.   Part-Song.
Smith, H. P.

If music be the food of love.
Benson, G.   Part-Song.

O mistress mine.
Baines, Herbert.   Song for Baritone (in a book of Six Songs).
Cardew, Herbert W.   Song for Baritone.
Daymond, E. R.
Davies, H. Walford.   Song for Tenor.
Drayton, H. U.   Song.
Gladstone, F. E.   Song for Baritone.

Johnson, Bernard. Song for Tenor.
MacCunn, H. Part-Song.
Macfarren, G. A.
Morley, T.
Needham, Alicia A. Song for Baritone.
Parry, C. H. H.
Richardson, A. M.
Smith, H. P.
Sullivan, Sir A.
Traditional. Song for Tenor. See *Three Shake-speare Songs* (A. E. Hull).
Vicars, G. R. Part-Song.
Waddington, S. P. Part-Song.
Walthew, Richard.
Wareing, H. W. Part-Song.
Young, W. J. Part-Song.

She never told her love.
Haydn. Song for Soprano.

When that I was and a tiny little boy.
Davies, H. Walford. Song for Tenor.
Wareing, H. W.

TWO GENTLEMEN OF VERONA

Who is Sylvia?
Bishop, H. R. Part-Song.
Bright, Dora.
German, E.
Ham, Albert. Part-Song.
Macfarren, G. A. Part-Song.
Macfarren, W. Part-Song.
Marks, T. Osborne.
Schubert, F. Song for Soprano or Tenor.
Young, W. J. Part-Song.

WINTER'S TALE

Jog on the foot-path way.
> Macirone, C. A.   Part-Song.

When daffodils begin to peer.
> Redman, Douglas.   Two-Part Song.
> Wareing, H. W.   Part-Song.

Will you buy any tape?
> Macirone, C. A.   Part-Song.
> Williams, C. Lee.   Part-Song.
> Fox, Arthur.   Incidental Music.

VENUS AND ADONIS

Bid me discourse.
> Bishop, H. R.   Song for Soprano.

E'en as the sun.
> Bishop, H. R.   Part-Song and Chorus.

PASSIONATE PILGRIM

Crabbed age and youth.
> Parry, C. H. H.   Song for Soprano or Tenor.
> Stevens, R. J. S.   Glee.

Good night, good rest.
> Bishop, H. R.   Part-Song.
> Macfarren, Walter.   Part-Song.

Come live with me, and be my love.
> Hamilton, E. W.   Part-Song.

SONNETS

As it fell upon a day.
> Bishop.
> Mornington, Earl of.   Glee.
> Reay, S.   Part-Song.

From you I have been absent all the Spring.
> Crossley, T. Hastings.   Duet.

No longer mourn for me when I am dead (The Triumph of Death).
> Holland, C.   Part-Song.
> Parry, C. H. H.   (In a set of Five Songs.)

Shall I compare thee.
> Parry, J. H.   Part-Song.

Claude Debussy is stated (1916) to be working on a piece entitled *King Lear.*